THE ANATOMY
OF A
TURNAROUND

GREG VIOLETTE

Printed in the United States of America

ISBN-10: 0-9983381-1-7

ISBN-13: 978-0-9983381-1-8

10 9 8 7 6 5 4 3 2

Empire Publishing

www.empirebookpublishing.com

FROM THE AUTHOR

You will see that this book contains the actual work product – all the reports, memos and charts – that I generated during the process of this turnaround project. I did this so the reader can visualize the process through my eyes, and get a sense of the timeline, as well as adding to the book's authenticity. At the end of each chapter, you will find the exhibits that pertain to the subject matter in that chapter.

My recent writing summarizes the entire project, from "The Introduction" to the owner (first chapter) to "The Closing" of the sale (last chapter). If you are only interested in the summary of a turnaround project, you may skip or skim the exhibits. However, those reports contain considerable relevant information regarding the allegations of misconduct, details of the plan, execution of the plan, the personalities involved; and they will give you valuable insight into the inner workings of this (or any) company.

If you are only interested in the principles for effective leadership and how to manage and motivate people, you can skip to the chapter titled "Step Three – Management Training", where I have outlined my philosophy called "Common Sense Management". In much of the rest of the book, you will learn how those principles were used to execute my plan.

If you are only interested in the finer points of labor cost reduction and improving operational efficiency, you can find those details in "Step Two – Reorganization and Workforce Reduction". Or you may want to focus on changing the culture of an organization, which is presented in the last step of the turnaround. There is a wide variety on the menu for you to choose from.

This book not only tells a story, it provides a wealth of valuable information to those that are interested in learning about the operations of a company and specifically how to fix problems. And there are those who may enjoy this book strictly because of the real life drama and behind-the-scenes activities that actually took place in this Nevada casino. Regardless of your background or interests, I think you will find some value in this book.

Contents

THE INTRODUCTION

"We thought Full House Resorts was ripe for a change in management."

Laughlin, Nevada is a desert town with about 7,000 residents on the Colorado River, 100 miles south of Las Vegas. With eleven casino/resorts lined up on the banks of the river, it's a mini Las Vegas, where you can step out the door of a casino and go for a boat ride. There are several thousand casino workers, and most of them live in Bullhead City, Arizona, population 40,000, on the other side of the river.

The River Palms Casino/Resort, where I directed the turnaround, is one of those eleven resorts, with 1,100 employees, 1,000 hotel rooms, 1200 slot machines, ten bars and restaurants, convention center, salon/spa and boat rentals. It is nestled between the Golden Nugget and Harrah's.

My introduction to the owner of the River Palms started with meeting Andre Hilliou, then Michael Paulson and Lee Iacocca. I partnered with Andre to find a casino management opportunity. He was the CEO of Vision Gaming in Atlanta, a slot machine manufacturing company. He wanted to get back into managing casinos. I was doing consulting work, which is what most unemployed executives do. I was just looking for a job. We were introduced by a mutual friend - a recruiter in the casino business.

1

We thought Full House Resorts was ripe for a change in management. It is a small public company based in Las Vegas. The stock was trading near an all-time low below $.50 a share. They only had three employees - CEO, CFO and VP of Development - overseeing two management contracts, with one about to end.

We found that Michael Paulson, Trustee of the Allen Paulson Estate, was the largest shareholder with 30% of the stock. Lee Iacocca owned 20% of the shares and Bill McComas (CEO) had 10%. There were about 1,000 shareholders, with nobody else owning more than 4%. Our plan was to convince Michael Paulson that there was a need to change management.

I was able to contact Michael; and since we both lived in Las Vegas, he agreed to meet in my office the next day. He was frustrated with the management team at Full House Resorts, and was receptive to a change. He expressed the need to get Lee Iacocca involved, and offered to set up a meeting.

A couple weeks later the four of us met. Andre flew into Los Angeles from the east coast, and we met the night before to finalize the strategy for our big pitch. We would propose that Andre and I would replace the current CEO and CFO. We would take minimal salaries and no contract, with their promise that if we turned things around, we would be rewarded with bonuses and stock grants - low risk, high reward for both sides.

Lee's mansion in Bel Air, behind walls and gates, was like nothing I'd seen before. His housekeeper showed us to the parlor, where Lee and Mike were waiting. Lee was very amiable, and did most of the talking. Lee's a salesman. He once told me that he made 56 TV commercials. Andre's a fast talker; "bullshit artist" might be a more accurate description. On the other side of that coin, Michael and I are more reserved. We let them do most of the talking.

Our proposal was mostly a review of our background and qualifications. Andre had extensive experience as a CEO of casinos and manufacturing companies, as well as Chairman of the Board of a small public gaming company. I had more than 20 years' experience as a CFO – the last ten with casinos. I had been involved in several start-up and turnaround projects.

Without offering any details, we promised that we would work hard to bring in new business, and do our best to increase shareholder value. That is investment community lingo for increasing the price of the stock, which is the only thing that matters to the owners.

Fortunately Lee, too, was already convinced that a management change was necessary. After our presentation he told us he was confident we could do the job, but then dropped the bombshell that Andre and I had not considered. He says, "You know that the two guys I have to fire are the other two Board members on a three-member Board... you think they will vote for your proposal?"

I felt a knot in my stomach, and Andre and I just stared at each other. There was a long silence before Michael said, "I need to get a seat on the Board." Lee quickly chipped in, "I think I can convince McComas (second Board member) that you should replace Shaughnessy (the CFO and third Board member). Since you are the largest shareholder, and your dad founded the company, it's only right that you have a seat on the Board. You and I will then have a majority of the votes."

Lee then explained to us that it might take some time to resolve this issue, before they could take further action on our proposal. However, he asked us to be patient, and he would get back to us when all the obstacles had been removed.

Back in the car Andre and I shared mixed emotions... happiness that we might have a great opportunity, and frustration that we are now removed from the process, with no control over what or when anything happens.

Andre and I did go to work for Lee, eventually, and it was a very successful venture for me. Working for Mr. Iacocca was one of the highlights of my career. Flying on a private plane with him and sitting alone with him in his office listening to him tell stories were experiences I'll never forget.

All my thoughts of Full House Resorts, however, quickly vanished the day after the meeting at Lee's home, when I got a phone call from Michael Paulson, and the first thing he said was, "I own this casino in Laughlin called the River Palms…"

THE OWNER

"When his father died, Michael found himself in charge of a billion-dollar empire, whether he wanted that responsibility or not."

To know Michael Paulson you have to understand that he grew up in Beverly Hills, the son of a self-made billionaire. Allen Paulson was an airplane mechanic in World War II. After the war he started building airplanes, and named his company Gulfstream. You've probably heard of that company - they sold small planes to individuals and corporations.

He sold his company to Chrysler for $880 million. That started his close friendship with Lee Iacocca, who was the Chairman of the Board of Chrysler at the time. I never met Allen Paulson, who died a couple years prior, but I was told that he was very gregarious, and he worked hard and played hard.

He also had an affinity for gambling, so when he sold Gulfstream he bought two casinos, first a small casino in Deadwood, South Dakota, then the Treasure Island, a riverboat in Biloxi, Mississippi. When he bought the Gold River Hotel and Casino in Laughlin, Nevada, he moved a giant pirate ship from the Treasure Island in Mississippi, and made it the centerpiece of the newly remodeled three-level casino. He added a 25-story hotel tower and changed the name to the River Palms Casino/Resort.

Allen liked sports in general and horse racing in particular, so he bought the Del Mar Country Club and Racetrack in Del Mar,

California and other horse breeding and training farms around the country. He owned a racehorse named Cigar, Horse of the Year in 1970. He had a life-size portrait of Cigar on a 15' by 30' tapestry that he hung on the wall in the Bingo Hall at the River Palms. He also had a personal collection of sports memorabilia displayed in the Sports Book.

Michael Paulson inherited his father's love of horses. The only time I ever saw Michael on national TV was when he was interviewed on NBC at the Kentucky Derby, because he owned a filly that was in the race.

Allen Paulson and Lee Iacocca hung out with Barron Hilton. Bill McComas, who made a fortune in hotels, was also a part of that group. They all had homes at a country club in Palm Springs. "I'm a rich man," Lee once said in a meeting with me, Michael and Andre, "but Allen Paulson had so much money, he made me look like a peasant."

One of Michael Paulson's best friends is Rick Hilton, son of Barron and father of Paris. Michael and Rick were childhood friends, because of their fathers' close friendship. Michael engaged Rick, then a commercial real estate broker in New York City, to sell the River Palms.

When Allen died, Michael found himself in charge of a billion-dollar empire, whether he wanted that responsibility or not. When I met him, he was obviously in a liquidation mode, selling off assets. The River Palms was probably one of the smaller assets that he was trying to sell.

Although he rarely revealed his feelings, he seemed to be overwhelmed, and didn't seem comfortable doing what he was doing. He complained a lot about lawyers. He had been trying to sell the River Palms, but couldn't find a buyer, because of poor cash flow. At the same time, he and his sisters were going through a messy battle against his stepmother in probate court. That consumed a lot of Michael's time.

THE INVESTIGATION

"The real investigative work was done off property, meeting with whistle blowers."

When Michael came to talk about the River Palms, he told me that he had received anonymous phone calls and letters from employees, reporting the misconduct of the General Manager and his executive staff. He suspected that there may be some payroll fraud, unauthorized expenditures and general mismanagement. He was most upset that he had been contributing $300,000 to $400,000 every quarter for the last two years, as capital contributions to fund continuing operations. A later peak at the balance sheet confirmed his contributions of more than $1 million a year.

I expressed my dismay that a casino/resort with more than $70 million in annual revenues and a location on the Colorado River could not generate a positive cash flow. Casinos in general are known to have higher profit margins than most other businesses.

Michael informed me that the resort had been for sale for quite a few months. He was asking $25 million, which I thought was relatively cheap, considering I was sure that Allen Paulson had invested more than that to expand and remodel the property. In the casino business, the sales price is usually based on a multiple of annual cash flow. You have to have a profitable operation to sell a casino, or justify the potential.

He said he had not responded to the anonymous employee complaints, because he expected the property to be sold, and the

8

new owners could deal with those problems. However, since he couldn't sell the property, he felt it was more urgent to fix the problems that were negatively affecting the cash flow.

Michael then asked me if I could perform an undercover investigation to determine if the allegations and his suspicions were accurate. My reply was, "Of course. I've done that type of thing before." That answer was partially true. I started my career as an operational auditor, and had performed many audits throughout my career. However, I had never done one undercover. But what the hell, I've watched a lot of crime shows. I didn't think it would be difficult.

I prepared an Engagement Letter (Exhibit 1), which outlined the scope of the project, based on Michael's suspicions, the anonymous complaints and my experience identifying opportunities for efficiency and profit improvement.

Michael approved the contract and alerted the Staff that I would be performing a routine audit. I completed the investigation during a three week period in November. The staff knew it wasn't a routine audit, since I didn't offer any credentials from an accounting firm or regulatory agency. And there was a lot of speculation as to the real purpose of my audit. When I was in the office I performed all the tasks that an auditor would, but the real investigative work was done off property, meeting with whistle blowers.

Michael gave me the name and number of one employee that signed their name to a complaint letter. I met with that person, and she made some serious allegations. She gave me the name of another person, who might be willing to talk to me, and he gave me the name of another person, and it continued like that until I had several confirmations of the same incidents and general conduct of the management team.

9

Each time I talked to someone for the first time, almost every one of them related at least one incident that I hadn't heard before. The list of allegations continued to grow. There were Gaming Regulatory violations, misappropriation of company funds/assets/resources, violations of company policy, conflicts of interest, favoritism, misconduct and mismanagement.

I learned early in my career as an auditor that you don't identify problems by reviewing documents. You find out where the problems are by talking to the employees, the lower their pay grad, the better. The front line employees know what the problems are, and are more willing to talk about them.

I had success as an auditor, because I was able to get information from people, that they hadn't intended to divulge, because I asked questions in a non-threatening way, tried to make them feel comfortable, and feel confident that their name would never be divulged.

In Exhibit 2, I outlined the operational deficiencies that were identified during my audit. In Exhibit 3, I reported a vast array of allegations of misconduct primarily against the General Manager and his immediate staff. If the allegations were true, I would expect the GM to be fired for gross negligence, gross misconduct and misappropriation of company assets. There was a lot of evidence. There were a lot of witnesses. The behavior was shocking to me. I had never seen or heard anything like it. I found out how a GM can turn a property into his own personal playground when there is absentee ownership.

In Exhibit 4, I summarized the misconduct allegations by category.

Exhibit 1

**Greg Violette
Consulting**

Memo

To: Michael Paulson

From: Greg Violette

CC:

Date: October 7, 2002

Re: River Palms Audit

My understanding is that you want a Payroll Audit and an Operations Audit. The Payroll Audit will ascertain whether there are any "ghosts" on the payroll. I will personally observe the distribution of all the payroll checks. Each employee receiving a check will be required to provide an employee badge and personal identification. The payroll will also be cross-checked to Personnel records to ensure that someone has not fraudulently obtained an employee identification badge or kept their badge after termination. I will also reconcile the payroll to the Personnel records to verify that each employee is being paid at the proper rate of pay. My arrival and the announcement of my involvement will have to be carefully planned to avoid any changes to the payroll before the checks are printed.

The Operations Audit will begin with a review of the Income Statement to determine if any expenses seem to be "out of line" based on the volume of business activity. That review will identify certain areas that require special attention. For example, calculating the food and beverage cost of sales ratios will indicate whether the pricing is high or low, or inventory is being wasted or stolen. Calculating Marketing expense as a percentage of revenue will determine if it is in an acceptable range.

The Operations Audit will include the following areas:

1) Staffing Levels – are they appropriate for each department based on the level of business activity?

2) Scheduling – are they practicing Demand Scheduling?

3) Marketing

1

a) Is there a busing program?

b) If so, what does it cost?

c) Are there adequate controls on cash receipts from customers at events at the events center and beach facilities?

d) Are they tracking the spending of the bus patrons?

e) Is there a Player Tracking System?

f) If so, is it being managed properly?

g) Is there a Rewards Program?

h) If so, are the rewards appropriate for the level of play?

i) Is the program being administered properly?

j) Is the cost of advertising appropriate considering the market and competition?

k) Are the advertising dollars being spent wisely?

l) Are the proper advertising mediums being used?

m) Is and ad agency being utilized?

n) Is it cost effective?

o) Certain aspects of marketing/advertising can either be done in-house or contracted out. I will determine if in-house work should be contracted out and vice versa.

4) Purchasing

a) Review the bidding process and procedures.

b) Test a sample of high dollar expenditures to determine if the appropriate bidding process was followed.

c) Review expenditures by vendor.

d) Are there any "ghost" vendors?

e) Are they receiving volume discounts?

f) Does the pricing seem to be appropriate?

g) Are all attempts being made to get the best possible pricing?

h) Are there adequate controls to ensure that nothing is being shipped directly to someone's home?

i) Are there adequate controls to ensure that goods and services are actually received before the invoices are paid?

j) Review the expenditure authorization procedures to determine if the appropriate individuals have the appropriate spending authorization levels.

5) Food and Beverage

a) Is the Pricing appropriate?

b) Is the quality acceptable?

c) Are there adequate controls over inventory?

d) Are there procedures in place to minimize waste?

6) Complimentaries

a) Is the total cost appropriate, based on the level of business activity?

b) Who has comping authority and what level? Are they appropriate?

c) Review historical data for evidence of abuse.

7) Credit and Collections

a) Are the credit policies too liberal or restrictive?

b) Are collections done in-house or do they use a service?

c) If it's done in-house, is it done diligently?

d) If they use a service, is it cost effective?

e) Review the Outstanding Receivables for abnormalities.

f) Are there any employees on the list?

g) Review bad debt write-offs

8) Cash Shortages

a) Are employees required to pay/reimburse shortages?

b) Are disciplinary measures taken for excessive or large shortages?

c) Are overs and shorts reported on a timely basis?

d) Are the employee change banks adequate but not excessive?

e) Is the Cage Bankroll adequate but not excessive?

f) Are cash reserves invested wisely?

9) Employee Payroll Advances

a) What is the policy?

b) Have there been any abuses?

10) Hotel Room Pricing – Is it based on customer demand and competition?

11) Internal Reporting – Is the system adequate to provide senior management with effective tools to properly manage the business?

12) Customer Service

a) Are employee's providing good service?

b) Evaluate the morale.

The focus of my review will be to identify actual or potential theft, fraud, abuse, neglect or mismanagement, and opportunities to improve efficiency and profitability. In my experience, if there are problems or opportunities, they are usually in the areas listed above. I will not attempt to determine the accuracy of the income statements or any other reports. My objective will be to identify problems and opportunities, and I will not attempt to implement any changes, only make recommendations in a written report. I expect this project to take approximately 15 working days, and my proposed fee is $10,000, payable upon completion and submission of my detailed report on the above statement of work. This fee will include periodic status reports and follow-up meetings to review findings with Michael Paulson. Assuming that my room and reasonable meal costs will be complimentary, I will not bill you for any expenses.

Respectively submitted by,

Gregory Violette

Gregory Violette, Consultant

Accepted by: _____

Michael Paulson ,
President, River Palms Hotel & Casino

Exhibit 2

GREG VIOLETTE
CONSULTING

2260 Surrey Meadows Avenue
Henderson, NV   89052

December 11, 2002

Michael Paulson
Gold River Hotel and Casino, Inc.
c/o Paulson Enterprises
P.O. Box 9660
Rancho Santa Fe, CA   92067

Dear Michael:

In accordance with the terms of our consulting agreement, I performed an operational audit of the River Palms Casino and Hotel during the period October 15 through November 13. I did not attempt to verify the accuracy of any of the financial information that was provided to me. That type of audit is done on an annual basis by a CPA firm, and also periodically by the Nevada Gaming Commission. The scope of my audit was outlined in my proposal. My primary objective was to identify operational deficiencies and profit improvement opportunities.

I started my review by analyzing income statements and other financial information, which identified areas of concern. A more in-depth analysis was then performed by interviewing approximately thirty employees from all levels of management in many different departments and reviewing pertinent documentation. The interviews focused primarily on procedures and controls.

The following is a history of revenues, cash flows and significant expense items for the last four years (in millions):

Year	Revenue	Cash Flow	Margin	Mktg	Comps
1999	60.7	4.1	6.8%	7.2	6.2
2000	71.3	4.1	5.8%	12.9	8.0
2001	68.1	2.3	3.4%	12.8	7.6
2002 (est)	74.7	4.1	5.5%	12.1	11.7

The year 2000 was Duff Taylor's first full year as General Manager. A quick review of this historical data reveals two disturbing facts – 1) The revenue in 2002 will be $14M higher than 1999, but the cash flow has not increased at all, and 2) A 5.5% cash flow margin is very low for any casino/hotel operation. It should be noted that the comps are a component of revenue, therefore the real cash revenue is calculated by subtracting Comps from Revenue.

According to Duff Taylor, he made some mistakes in marketing the property – spent too much in 2000, cut back too far in 2001, and spent too much again in 2002. My observation is that, in three years, he still hasn't figured out how to market the property. He has been "buying" additional revenue, but none of it is dropping to the bottom line.

Financial information for the other properties in Laughlin is very difficult to find, therefore I consulted with a friend of mine, John Lind, who has been the CFO at Ramada Express for seven years. According to him, there are four properties in Laughlin which generate more than $75M in annual revenues, with the Riverside being the highest at $125M. John believes that those four properties, including his own, have cash flow margins ranging from the high teens to mid-twenties. In his opinion, the River Palms (without knowing the revenue), should have a cash flow margin between 12% and 15%. Those percentages are quite low for the gaming industry. A 12% cash flow margin at the River Palms translates to almost $9M. My conclusion, based on this information and other factors listed below, is that the River Palms is seriously under-performing.

Other factors that contribute to the low cash flow margin at the River Palms include the physical condition of the property, and the fact that the casino has multiple levels. These factors contribute to an otherwise inefficient operation.

In my opinion, the cash flow at the River Palms, with good management should be at least $6M, with the potential to get to $8M and higher with additional capital investments. This could be achieved by cutting the marketing expense by $1.5M, reducing labor expense by $1.5M, and reducing other expenses by $1M with smart management and increased efficiencies.

In a review of marketing expenses with John Strickland, VP of Marketing, he "offered up" a $1M reduction, which I believe has already been incorporated in the 2003 budget. In addition to that, I believe there is another $500,000 in potential savings in marketing.

A review of the employee headcounts for October, 2002, revealed that there are 64 more employees than the same time last year. This translates to approximately $1.5M in payroll and related expenses. I believe the operation could be streamlined to reduce the employee headcount to the same level as last year, which was 995.

The operation is very top heavy, with too many VP's, directors, assistant managers, assistant supervisors, etc. Some of these positions could be eliminated, with a streamlining of the operation.

Other operational deficiencies include the following:

1) Budgets – Front line managers do not play an active role in developing their own budgets, and are not held accountable for keeping their expenses within budget.

2) Comps – Not properly controlled. For example, every salaried employee has a "comp bank", and is allowed to comp friends and family. This is considered an employee benefit, which is unheard of in the industry. There are more than 150 employees with comping privileges.

3) Systems Implementation – Implementation of new systems has not been properly planned and coordinated. Some employees complained that the old player tracking system was better than the new one. Not enough employees who are intimately involved with the system were consulted in the design and implementation of the new system.

4) Accounts Receivable – Collections of bad checks and markers could be increased with the use of collection agencies.

5) Cash Handling – Controls over cash ticket sales at special events are lacking. For example, the same person printed the tickets, sold the tickets, and deposited the cash for the Paul Anka concert, with no independent reconciliation.

6) Consultants – The need for, and value received from, some consultants is questionable.

My findings and recommendations are opinions and judgments based on the review of documentation and employee interviews. These findings were not reviewed with casino management.

Sincerely,

Greg Violette
Consultant

Exhibit 3

**GREG VIOLETTE
CONSULTING**

2260 Surrey Meadows Avenue
Henderson, NV   89052

December 11, 2002

Michael Paulson
Gold River Hotel and Casino, Inc.
c/o Paulson Enterprises
P.O. Box 9660
Rancho Santa Fe, CA   92067

Dear Michael:

In conjunction with my operational audit, you asked me to investigate an employee allegation of management wrongdoings in the hiring of consultants. You also indicated that you had received anonymous letters from employees with complaints about management. You gave me the name of an employee that I should contact on a confidential basis.

I conducted an initial interview with that employee, and received a number of allegations against Duff Taylor, the General Manager. So as not to arise any suspicions, I kept the interview short, but followed up with a phone interview at the employee's home. That employee gave me the name of another employee who would be willing to substantiate the allegations. I conducted a short interview with that employee then had a meeting with both employees off property. They gave me the name of a third employee who would be willing to further substantiate the allegations. I conducted a lengthy interview with that employee. All three related virtually the same incidents of Duff Taylor's inappropriate behavior and mismanagement.

Two of these employees are managers and the third is a director. The average tenure with the company of these three employees is ten years. I believe the allegations to be credible. Another salaried employee, who is very close to Duff Taylor, asked to speak to me in private, and did not volunteer any information about Duff's personal behavior, but made the same allegations as the others about poor management.

All four employees volunteered information contingent upon my promise of confidentiality and assurance that their names would never be revealed to anyone. All four feared retribution. As justification for that fear, the following was related to me. Duff Taylor was given a letter by Mike Paulson. It was an anonymous letter from an employee about preferential treatment. Duff was livid, and conducted an investigation to determine who sent the letter. Also, an engineer wanted to write a letter to Mr. Paulson, but the executive office would not give him the address. And finally, Duff's secretary recently sent an email to all VP's and Directors, instructing them not to give out Mr. Paulson's address or phone number to any employees.

The following is a summary of the information I received from the first three employees:

Duff Taylor is not well-respected by most of the employees at the River Palms. The personal behavior of he and some of his immediate staff is not what you would normally expect from people in high profile positions. Some of the terms used by the employees to describe these executives were "unprofessional", "lack of integrity", "lack of respect" and "lacking morals and ethics". The allegations include possible violations of company policy, gaming regulations and federal labor laws. There may have been sexual harassment, and some of their actions could also be defined as abuse of power and misappropriation of company assets and funds. Duff Taylor has made this property a "personal playground" for he and his immediate staff, and they have abused the authority they have been given.

One of the reasons that Duff is not respected is because of the preferential treatment that he gives to his "inner circle" and a select few others. Top management gets all the perks. They get bigger raises than the hourly employees. Management often preaches one thing, but does another.

Duff's credibility has also been questioned, especially when he tells everybody in meetings that "we're millions ahead of last year", yet they can't pay their bills on time. There are quite a few vendors who are unhappy with the River Palms, because of late payments.

Most of the issues directly affect Duff's personal integrity and professionalism. His personal behavior compromises his ability to enforce policies. Policy enforcement is inconsistent, depending on the personal relationship that he has with the individuals involved.

The following are some examples of incidents that have created the perceptions noted above:

Duff is a married man, with a home in Las Vegas, and his wife lives there. He also has a girlfriend living with him in his suite at the River Palms. This is common knowledge among all the employees. Caroline was a cocktail waitress at the Riverside when they met. All of Caroline's meals and drinks are comped. Duff has given the PBX operators specific instructions on how to handle calls from his wife. Duff's wife once confronted a housekeeper, asking her if she had ever seen another woman in the room. Caroline has to "move out" of Duff's room, when his wife is in town.

Duff and Caroline are often seen together on property. They have dinner together at Madeleines almost every night. They have been known to get drunk and create a scene. A VIP customer once complained about Duff and Caroline being drunk and arguing in the booth next to his at Madeleines. Caroline has been known to be rude

19

to employees, primarily in Housekeeping and in Madeleines. She has quite often been seen drunk in Madeleines by herself.

They have often been seen together walking together through the casino, carrying a glass of wine. Duff has been known to squeeze her ass in full view of the customers and employees.

Caroline drives Duff's company vehicle when he is out of town. One night she went to O'Leary's Tavern in Bullhead City and got drunk. A security officer from the River Palms went to pick her up, and another employee picked up the company vehicle.

Duff is President of the Laughlin Tourism Committee. A city official commented about Duff bringing his girlfriend to a public event – how inappropriate it was - when it was common knowledge that he has a wife in Las Vegas. There have been at least three "public" events that Duff and Caroline attended. It was reported that they were both drunk at one of them.

Caroline gets preferential treatment around the property. The River Palms gave the Mohave News more advertising business, because Caroline was selling advertising for them. Right now Caroline is selling cell phones to River Palms employees, despite the company's "No Solicitation" policy.

Recently, Duff staged a birthday party for Caroline at the River Palms, and invited the top management employees and their spouses. He closed the Pool area on a Saturday night, and the casino supplied the food, drinks, cooks, bartenders and servers.

There have been many parties like this for Duff and his immediate staff, paid for by the company, but of questionable benefit to the company. One in particular was on the Colorado Belle's "yacht" and included strippers. These parties always include free food and drinks.

Early last year, they brought in an all-girl band from Las Vegas to perform in the Bermuda Club. After the show, Duff Taylor, Charley Christy, Wright Wilson and Dean Bridge locked the door and had a private party with the band. The Surveillance Operator reported to the Shift Manager that Charlie was performing oral sex on one of the girls as she sat on top of the bar. Duff was dancing with another band member who had removed her top. The Shift Manager contemplated knocking on the door, but decided to do nothing, because of his fear of retribution.

There are currently 11 pending EEOC claims of harassment or discrimination, specifically naming Duff Taylor and Ed Ortiz (Beverage Manager), all filed within the last three months. Previous to that there was only one claim in the last five years. The complaints are all from cocktail servers. One of the women, who has a complaint pending, actually received a large settlement (two years pay) in the year 2000 for a similar complaint.

Duff has been quoted as saying he wants the cocktail servers to be young, slender and attractive. He changed the uniforms, and much of the uproar has to do with some of the women not wanting, or not being able to, wear them. They also have to be able to fit into them, with a maximum size limitation. There have also been allegations of preferential treatment in scheduling shifts and work areas for the cocktail servers, which directly affect their tips.

Recently, Duff invited all the Vice Presidents, Directors, selected Managers, and their significant others (36 people) to a party on the Company's "yacht". They were on the boat for four hours, then they were in Madeleines for another four hours. They were drinking the whole time. A lot of people got drunk, and some of them came back into the Casino. Fred Naugle, the Table Games Manager, was drunk and staggering and went into the pit, was verbally abusive and intimidating to other employees. He was suspended almost immediately. Since then many of the dealers have come forward with complaints of harassment and intimidation by Fred Naugle. The company hired an attorney to sort out the facts and assist with the case. The final result was that Fred did not get fired, and it could very well be that Duff's personal involvement with Fred, and the fact that Duff organized the party where Fred got drunk, were factors in the decision not to fire Fred.

Rose Thompson is the Vice President of Human Resources. Her husband (Gerard) was hired as a consultant in the Food and Beverage Departments after he lost his job at the Riverside. Some casinos do not allow Human Resources and Surveillance employees to have an immediate family member working anywhere in the casino. His assignment did not last very long, because he was seriously injured in a motorcycle accident in January of this year.

Rose Thompson received full pay for four months, while she was attending to her husband after the accident. She didn't work at all during that period, and was never placed on any kind of leave of absence. Then for another two months, while receiving full pay, she worked maybe one day a week. It gradually increased to three and four days a week, but it was October before she actually put in a full week. Now, after nine months, she is still not working full time, because of the care that her husband needs. There were a few occasions when Rose brought Gerard to work with her, and he stayed in a hotel room while she worked. That proved to be very disruptive, because of the constant attention that he needs. Rose claims that she has been working from home, but that is not true.

Employees have been terminated for expiring LOA's, including one person who had 13 years of service. The preferential treatment given to Rose Thompson is resented by other employees.

This organization is very top heavy, and the people at the top never seem to be around. High level employees have received full pay during lengthy absences. Some of them include Dave Scranton, Charlie Christy, Dean Bridge, Travis Carrico and Harry Cox. It was usually explained that they were on business for Mr. Paulson.

There is a fraternization policy that prohibits supervising another employee if they are dating. Wright Wilson's (Chief Financial Officer) girlfriend, who lives with him in his River Palms suite, was his secretary when they started dating. They carried on quite overtly for about a year, before she transferred to the Gift Shop as a part time employee.

Fred Sayre, Director of Surveillance, and a married man, is dating a dealer, and there are at least three supervisors in the pit that are dating dealers. Rob Petit is a Shift Manager, and his wife is a dealer, but on a different shift. Management is enforcing the policy on a selective basis, which puts the company at a liability.

Wright Wilson and Dean Bridge (VP, Slots) have suites in the hotel. Joey D'Angelo, who owns the Italian Restaurant, also lived in the hotel for quite awhile, but probably not any longer. John Hastings, who is a high roller and a friend of Jimmy Glover, one of the shift managers, had a room in the hotel for about six months. The owner of Dream Girls, a strip joint in Bullhead City, lives in the hotel. Charlie Christy, former Assistant GM, lived in the hotel for a lengthy period. An elderly woman (that Charlie called "Aunt Patty") also lived in the hotel for almost a year. We believe all these were/are comped rooms.

Charlie Christy was originally brought in as Assistant General Manager. He used to disappear for weeks at a time. They kept changing his title, and he kept getting raises. His status was then changed to Consultant, and he continued to get paid after he left.

Dave Scranton was Director of Security for two years. It seemed like he never worked. He wouldn't be seen him for weeks at a time. During "Harley Weekend" the busiest weekend of the year, Dave was seen off property on a Saturday afternoon.

There was a promotion awhile back that involved a drawing for a boat. The more you played, the more coupons you would get. John Hastings won the drawing. It was common knowledge that he had thousands of coupons. It was also common knowledge that his roommate, Jimmy Glover (one of the shift managers), stole the coupons and gave them to John. They let him keep the boat, and Jimmy Glover is still employed.

Another drawing (PT Cruiser) was won by the wife of Lyn Nusom, the Manager of Madeleines. It was alleged that they were separated, and therefore she was able to keep the car, but it was proven later that they were very married. There is a policy prohibiting employees and their family members from participating in drawings.

David Coffey, owner of the Gift Shop and Arcade, has won a lot of cash prizes (several thousand dollars). After complaints from other customers, an audit confirmed that he and his wife and Doug Wykoff had an inordinate number of coupons in the drum.

Duff Taylor, Dean Bridge, and Dave Scranton have invested in a racetrack in Indiana that is adding a casino. They will have the management contract for the casino. Dean Bridge has a proposed layout of the casino hanging on the wall in his office. It is very likely that they have spent considerable time planning this project. They may have used company funds to pay for trips to that property.

On several occasions Dave Scranton (Security Director) took duffle bags full of cash from the cage. Supposedly, this cash was taken to the bank to cover accounts payable checks or payroll. This was usually done very late on a Friday afternoon. It appeared that nobody else accompanied Dave to the bank (if it was still open). It probably left the cage short of the minimum bankroll requirements. The prior Cage Manager resigned because of this practice.

There are conflicts between some departments that work together, but don't report to the same person. For example, the hotel reservations staff reports to the VP of Marketing, and the front desk personnel report to a different VP. Also, the banquet organizers report to the VP of Marketing, and the banquet servers report to the Food and Beverage Department.

One Saturday night near the end of October Duff Taylor's son created a scene in the casino, when he punched his girlfriend in the face. The two had to be separated by security officers, and the situation was resolved by providing one of them with a separate room in the hotel.

The first three employees that were interviewed all separately volunteered that they believed the unprofessional conduct related above was due to the lack of a presence on property by the owners, and that senior management was taking advantage of the situation. They also all separately volunteered that Duff Taylor's behavior had changed dramatically, since I initiated my review.

The following are some general statements made by the four employees that they all seem to agree on:

There is a serious morale problem among the hourly employees. They are "treated like garbage". They only get "lip service" – promises, but no action, when it comes to resolving their complaints.

There is no follow-up on customer complaints. Employee complaint letters are often just ignored.

Favoritism is rampant in hiring, firing, scheduling, disciplinary action and dealing with poor performance and lack of competency. There are double standards – one set of rules for some people, and a different set of rules for others.

23

There is reluctance on the part of top management to "get into the trenches". They avoid dealing with lower level employees.

There is very little effort to select the right people for jobs and promotions. For example, there is a young guy with an MBA and a lot of talent, who is doing data entry work. On the other side of the coin, there is a supervisor in Food and Beverage, making $38,000 a year, who can't even write a business letter.

Employee turnover is very high – 62% on an annualized basis this year. Most people come in with a good positive attitude, then they leave after three to six months, when they find out what it really is like to work here.

Some employees have gone too far with the Casual Day (Fridays). Some management employees wear faded jeans and t-shirts. One guy was even seen wearing bib overalls.

Duff Taylor is too nice. He doesn't hold people accountable for good performance. His attitude is "let the managers manage". People take advantage of him. A lot of the managers have a poor work ethic. They come in late, leave early, take a lot of time off, and are not productive when they are at work. They have no accountability.

I talked to several dealers, while I was posing as a customer playing blackjack. One of them with 17 years at River Palms, when asked what she thinks about the current management team, replied "too much favoritism". She said the management was better when the property was owned by Boyd Gaming.

The four employees suggested that some of the other issues that should be investigated include: 1) part time employees may be receiving benefits they are not entitled to, 2) some full time employees are not working enough hours to qualify for the benefits they are receiving, 3) for some period of time, the employee contributions to the 401K plan weren't getting deposited on a timely basis, because the company was using the funds to help alleviate a cash flow problem, 4) overtime is excessive and given to select individuals, and 5) the company paid a $40,000 "reinstatement fee" to Nevada Care, because of late payments for the employees' health insurance.

I have some documentation to substantiate some of these last allegations. I did not confront senior management with any of the allegations. Please be reminded that I must protect the identity of these four employees at all costs.

Sincerely,

Greg Violette
Consultant

24

Exhibit 4

ALLEGATIONS by CATEGORY

GAMING VIOLATIONS

1) Duff Taylor's son (Jason) was being paid for training without a Sheriff's Card
2) Cash Drawings were "rigged". Management was aware of it, but did nothing about it
3) Cash was removed from the Cage without the proper controls, and without following standard procedures

CONFLICT OF INTEREST

Micro Gaming Technologies is a company owned by Duff Taylor, Wright Wilson, Dean Bridge, Travis Carrico and Mark Bryant. This company is doing business with the River Palms, and has received substantial payments for services and equipment.

MISAPPROPRIATION OF COMPANY FUNDS/ASSETS/RESOURCES

1) Birthday parties for Duff and his girlfriend (Caroline Henry) on company property with food and beverages paid for by the company, using servers who were "on the clock"
2) An elaborate Christmas party (15-20 people) for Caroline's employer (Mohave Wireless) hosted by the River Palms, that was either comped or· done for a very minimum payment, below market standards
3) Use of a company vehicle by Duff's girlfriend
4) Personal loans to employees – Wright Wilson, Dean Bridge, John Strickland
5) Abuse of comping authority (Caroline)
6) Pursuing personal investments for personal gain on company time and at company expense
7) Personal travel expenses paid by the company

VIOLATIONS OF COMPANY POLICY

1) Leave of Absence policy (Rose Thompson)
2) EEOC claims of harassment and discrimination
3) Allowing employee fraternization
4) No Solicitation Policy
5) Nepotism

MISCONDUCT

1) Cohabitation of a married man with another woman on company property
2) Adultery
3) Flaunting of the above
4) Abuse of power
5) Favoritism/preferential treatment
6) Hiring strippers for a company party
7) Fraternization of a sexual nature on company property
8) Lying to employees and owner
9) Insubordination

MISMANAGEMENT

1) Late payment to the company's health insurance carrier, which resulted in considerable expense and problems
2) General poor work ethic at all levels within the company
3) Poor morale
4) High turnover
5) Poor treatment of low level employees
6) Poor follow-up of customer complaints
7) Poor follow-up of employee complaints
8) Favoritism
9) Over-staffing
10) Lack of teamwork
11) Waste
12) Poor financial results

THE REALITY:
NOW I HAVE TO FIX IT

"The whole management team was complicit"

Not long after Michael received my reports, he called me. Michael is not the excitable type - very low key. He didn't react the way most owners would when they found out they had been taken advantage of. But he did say he had to get Duff Taylor out of there.

I advised that my report might not have any standing in court, since I'm not a licensed investigator. I suggested that he suspend Duff, initiate a formal investigation by a licensed investigator, and put me in charge temporarily until Duff was exonerated or replaced. I told him that nothing would change until he replaced Duff with someone from the outside, because the whole management team was complicit.

On November 22, I informed Michael of a report I received of further misconduct and frivolous spending not previously reported (see Exhibit 5).

I submitted my proposed consulting agreement to Michael on November 27 (see Exhibit 6).

On January 3, I conveyed to Michael another report of disturbing behavior and previously unreported incidents (see Exhibit 7).

On January 18, I reported more disturbing news from the River Palms (see Exhibit 8).

On January 20, Michael signed my consulting contract (see Exhibit 9).

Exhibit 5

greg violette

From: "greg violette" <gviovegas@lvcm.com>
To: "Michael Paulson" <JMICHAELPA@aol.com>
Sent: Friday, November 22, 2002 8:57 PM
Subject: Duff Taylor

Mike,

I just got a call from one of our "informants" at the River Palms. She just came from having drinks with Caroline at The Lodge.

She re-confirmed, with Caroline, that she still lives in the hotel.

But this one takes the cake........Tomorrow night Caroline is hosting a party for her company, Mohave Wireless, in the Private Dining Room at The Lodge. There will be 16 or 17 people. They are having lobster, shrimp, Dom Perignon, etc., at a total cost of about $4,000. The whole dinner is being comped, even though Duff won't even be there. He is at home in Vegas this weekend.

Duff is planning his third anniversary party (three years of employment at the River Palms). It will be sometime very soon on the Company boat, and it will be the same as the last one, when Fred Naugle got in big trouble.

Duff announced at the Manager's Meeting today that he has purchased two vibrating recliners for $6,000 each to be placed in the casino, and customers will be able to sit in it for $1.00. They are planning to buy as many as six of these chairs. They brought one into the meeting for a demonstration. A lot of the people in the meeting walked out asking each other, "Do we want our customers sitting in recliners, or sitting at the slot machines?"

The informants seem to be very anxious to report these examples of Duff's misconduct, because they really think it is criminal the way he is taking advantage of the company, and they really want you to know.

Greg

1/18/2003

29

Exhibit 6

greg violette

From: "greg violette" <gviovegas@lvcm.com>
To: "Michael Paulson" <JMICHAELPA@aol.com>
Sent: Monday, January 13, 2003 6:35 PM
Subject: Fw: Proposal

Mike,

Here is the proposal I originally submitted on November 27.

I look forward to monitoring the activities at the River Palms to ensure that the operation is run smoothly, and provide the leadership that is required in the absence of a general manager.

Greg
----- Original Message -----
From: greg violette
To: Michael Paulson
Sent: Wednesday, November 27, 2002 3:24 PM
Subject: Proposal

Mike,

Since you seem to be leaning towards a suspension for Duff Taylor, and considering me to fill in until the investigation is complete, and considering that I do not yet have a Nevada Gaming License, I propose the following, based on my experience in such matters:

If it is a suspension, rather than termination, it would not be appropriate to put me on the payroll. I would continue to work as a consultant. I would not have the General Manager title. It would be Owner's Representative, or just Consultant. I would act as an advisor and custodian of the business.

I would:

1) Have daily contact and weekly meetings with the General Manager's staff, to ensure that the day to day operation of the business is handled properly.

2) Fix problems that I have already identified, with the current staff actually implementing changes.

3) Further investigate potential problems, and take corrective action on any new findings (through current staff).

4) Review and modify the 2003 Business Plan

5) Keep you informed of key issues.

6) Facilitate the investigation, by arranging confidential interviews between investigator(s) and informants.

I would not:

1) Have authority over, or a direct reporting relationship with, current staff members.

2) Sign checks or markers.

3) Implement my "Turnaround Plan".

My proposed consulting fee would be $800 a day, with no bonuses or other incentives, and no benefits, except for

1/18/2003

30

a room in the hotel and comped meals. I would start immediately (as soon as next Tuesday or Wednesday), and would commit to five days a week, including some weekends.

I need to remind you that I have promised confidentiality to the "informants", and therefore would advise you not to give Duff Taylor a copy of my report, or even show it to him, because he could possibly determine the source of some of the information.

I look forward to hearing from you on this issue, and assisting you with "righting the ship".

Greg Violette

1/18/2003

31

Exhibit 7

greg violette

From: "greg violette" <gviovegas@lvcm.com>
To: "Michael Paulson" <JMICHAELPA@aol.com>
Sent: Friday, January 03, 2003 1:28 PM
Subject: River Palms

Mike,

Got another report this morning from one of our "informants". Apparently Duff Taylor hasn't been on property in about two weeks. However, he has hired another consultant, at $7,500 a week, to "control labor expenses". This is a real joke. If a GM can't control labor costs, he shouldn't be in the position.

It's just another case of Duff filling the pockets of one of his "friends". Apparently there are now five consultants being paid by the River Palms.

The Christmas party for Caroline's company went off as planned. They were billed a small amount for an extravagant affair. And she is driving Duff's company vehicle while is out of town.

There are now 1130 employees on payroll. That is 65 more than I reported in October, and 125 more than October, 2001. That equates to an increase of aproximately $3 million in payroll and benefits expense.

According to the Hotel Manager, the weekly write-off for Duff's room (movies, phone calls and room service) is $2,000. Duff's compensation, when you include all of his "perks" is probably around $300,000.

Apparently, all of the "shenanigans" ceased when I was on property. Now it is back to business as usual, with Duff operating the property like it is his own personal playground, to the personal benefit of he and his immediate staff.

Sorry to have to be the bearer of all the bad news, but thought you would want to know.

Greg

1/18/2003

Exhibit 8

Greg Violette Consulting

Memo

To: Michael Paulson

From: Greg Violette

Date: January 18, 2003

Re: Addendum to Report

Two new confidential sources have volunteered additional information about the activities of Duff Taylor and his staff at the River Palms. One of the sources is a vice president and the other is a director. I consider them to be credible sources. The following is a summary of the information they have provided:

1) Duff Taylor, Wright Wilson, Dean Bridge, Travis Carrico and Mark Bryant own a company called Microtechnology. It is a software development company that has designed a kiosk-based player tracking system. Microtechnology has been providing services to the River Palms, and has received more than $150,000 in payments from them, through a consulting agreement with Mark Bryant.

2) Wright Wilson cashed a personal check at the Cage for $5,000, and asked them to "hold" it. After several weeks the check is still being "held", which would constitute an unauthorized loan.

3) Dean Bridge has received several cash advances, which have not been repaid. Normally, these advances would be repaid through the expense reporting process, or through payroll deductions. The purpose of the advances was not reported to me, however, the fact that they haven't been repaid on a timely basis raises suspicion.

4) Duff Taylor recently employed his son as an "Apprentice" in the Table Games Department. This is the young man who punched his girlfriend in the casino a couple months ago. I was told that he has visible tattoos and long dangling earrings, and works in the Pit. It is not known if, or how, he is being paid, but it was verified that he is not on the payroll. If he is being paid, it is through accounts payable.

5) Three more consultants have been hired in the past thirty days.

6) Duff Taylor has a "hidden room" in his hotel suite, where he hides Caroline's clothes, when his wife or children come to visit.

We now have several confidential "informants", who are key employees at the River Palms. They appear to be very dedicated and conscientious, and have a genuine interest in the success of the company. They are disgusted with the behavior and activities of the general manager and a couple of his immediate staff members. They have also expressed a high level of frustration with the appearance that nothing is being done about it.

1

CONSULTING AGREEMENT

This Consulting Agreement is made and entered into this 20th day of January, 2003, by and between Gold River Hotel and Casino, Inc. (Client) and Greg Violette (Consultant).

WHEREAS, Client's General Manager at the River Palms Casino and Hotel has been placed on a leave of absence, pending an investigation into his business practices and personal behavior, and Client has hired a Private Investigator to conduct aforementioned investigation, and Client has a need for management oversight during the absence of the General Manager; and

WHEREAS, Consultant has performed a preliminary investigation and reported allegations of the General Manager's misconduct by confidential employee informants, and Consultant is the only person who knows the identity of confidential informants, and Consultant has the necessary skills and experience to oversee the operation of the business;

NOW, THEREFORE, in consideration of the items listed below, the parties agree to the following:

CONSULTANT will perform the following services:
1) Assist Private Investigator in his investigation.

2) Oversee the operation of the business during the absence of the General Manager. Consultant's specific responsibilities for management oversight will be:

    A) Michael Paulson will serve as Acting General Manager, and Consultant will be Mr. Paulson's On-Site Representative. Consultant will implement changes only through Mr. Paulson or the Assistant General Manager with Mr. Paulson's approval.
    B) Work with Staff in all areas of strategic planning and day to day operation of the business.
    C) Fix problems previously identified and reported, with current staff actually implementing changes.
    D) Further investigate potential problems, and take corrective action on any new finding through current staff.
    E) Review and modify the 2003 Business Plan.
    F) Provide Weekly Activity Reports to Mr. Paulson.
    G) Consultant's primary responsibility will be to advise and recommend, and will not have authority over any employees, and will not sign any official documents.

A **CONSULTING FEE** of $4,000 per week will be paid to Consultant, based on a minimum of 40 hours per week, including travel time for one or two round trips home (Henderson) per week. Some work may be performed on weekends, depending on the demands of the business. Consultant will be provided a room in the hotel, meals in any of the food outlets, and incidental charges to his room (movies, phone calls, etc.) will also be comped. Client will be billed on a weekly basis, and invoices will be paid within ten working days.

This Agreement will be effective at the time of signing, and can be terminated by either party at any time with one week's notice.

AGREED TO AND ACCEPTED BY AND ON BEHALF OF:

BY: _Greg Violette_   DATE: _1/20/03_
     CONSULTANT

BY: _____   DATE: _1-20-03_
GOLD RIVER HOTEL & CASINO, Inc.

STEP ONE – STOP THE BLEEDING

"All nine items identified as remedies for the bleeding were implemented in the first two weeks."

I had been waiting many years for this opportunity - to be the top guy in the organization. I was well prepared. Since I had been dreaming about it for years, and visualized myself in the position, I had a lot of confidence.

Since I had been the number two guy in a lot of companies, I had worked for some good GM's and some bad ones. I learned how to do things right, and how to do them wrong, what works, and what doesn't. I was ready for the challenge. I was excited and highly motivated. I had been working on a strategic plan (in my mind) since I performed the investigation two months earlier.

I knew it was important to quickly establish my authority. I automatically got respect because I was representing the owner. But Wright Wilson would be running the day to day operations, with all of the Directors reporting to him, and I thought the line was kind of blurry as to who was really "in charge". Besides that, I strongly suspected that Wright would like to be the permanent GM, if Duff Taylor was terminated. I expected him to be lobbying for it. I also did not trust him, considering his past behavior. I had to set the tone immediately.

I had a private meeting with Wright Wilson, where I explained that there were many employees that thought he was part of the problem. "The perception of many is that putting you in charge won't change anything," I explained. I told him there were serious allegations against him personally, and I did not know how the investigator and Michael were going to handle it. That got his attention. I suggested that his future with the company might be based on my recommendation, and it would be in his best interest to be supportive of me and my efforts.

In the first Executive Staff meeting I reiterated what I had conveyed to Wright. All of the Executive Staff would report to Wright Wilson for routine matters involving the day to day operations, and they would take direction from me in implementing all the changes resulting from the Turnaround Plan.

I emphasized that Wright would be reporting to me and Michael Paulson. I explained that, "This is a temporary situation until Duff Taylor's case is resolved and either he is reinstated or another General Manager is appointed. Until then, I'm going to lead you in turning this company around."

That made it very clear who was in charge, and it became common knowledge among the employees. Boy did Wright Wilson jump on board. He dove in head first! He was very cooperative, very deferential, certainly had me convinced that he was supporting me 100%. He was not defensive about any of the changes I was proposing - smart guy!

I realized within a few days that it would not be practical for me to get Michael's approval for all the changes I was making, and I got the distinct impression that he did not want to be involved in details. So early on I decided that I was just going to forge ahead doing what I thought was necessary, and I would communicate with Michael frequently, so that he would be well aware of my actions. I assumed that if he didn't like what I was doing, he would let me know.

My first two reports to Michael Paulson after one week on the job are shown below as Exhibits 10 and 11.

At the end of week two I revealed my Assessment of the Property (Exhibit 12) and Strategic Turnaround Plan (Exhibit 13), which was very well received by the executive staff.

I also pointed out that the first phase of the Plan, "Stop the Bleeding", had already been completed. All nine items identified as remedies for the bleeding were implemented in the first two weeks. The management team seemed to be gratified, since we did that as a team, and everybody participated (Exhibit 14).

Exhibit 10

**GREG VIOLETTE
CONSULTING**

Memo

To: Michael Paulson

From: Greg Violette

CC:

Date: January 25, 2003

Re: Activity Report – Week of January 20, 2003

Below is my Activity Report for my first week on the job. The more I learn, the more time I spend on site, the more I am convinced that this operation is totally dysfunctional, and the spending is out of control.

Duff Taylor is not the right general manager for this property. He allowed the labor costs to get out of control, capital spending out of control, marketing expense out of control, comps out of control, not to mention his abuse of power, misconduct, misappropriation of funds and assets, etc. His priorities were misplaced and he had no focus on maximizing profits. He created a whole layer of upper management (VP's), so that he could spend more time on development projects and new business ventures.

It's interesting to watch all the executives distancing themselves from Duff Taylor. It's like watching people abandon a sinking ship. They were willing to accept the perks and participate in the shenanigans, but are now blaming him for all the problems, claiming ignorance and lack of participation in the decision making process.

1/20 - Meeting with Mike Paulson and Wright Wilson.

     Staff Meeting

     Marketing mtg – discuss technical problems with Rewards Program

1

1/21 - Meeting with Wright Wilson regarding Consultants

Discussed personal company loan with John Strickland

Analyzed cell phone expense – eliminated two people from the list

Prepared "Summary of Allegations" – 2 page report for Joe Dorsey

1/22 - Attended Staff Meeting with VP's and Directors

Meeting with Wright Wilson on financing issues

Meeting with Fred Sayre regarding allegations against Duff Taylor

Meeting with Joe Dorsey to discuss investigation

Contacted potential financing sources to refinance existing debt

1/23 - Reviewed files on Animal Habitat

Made phone calls regarding transfer of signs from Copa Casino

Preliminary conversations regarding refinancing of existing debt

Attended meeting on Customer Service Standards

1/24 - Lengthy meeting with Wright Wilson on a variety of issues

Cancelled Pat Cruzen consulting agreement

Met with Don Wiggington – IS Consultant

Further conversations with Fred Sayre re: Duff Taylor

Cancelled/postponed purchase of 50 PC/TV's ($65,000)

Delivered documentation (his request) to Joe Dorsey in Las Vegas

Next week I will focus on marketing expense, the "Balloon" project and other proposed capital expenditures, interview two more consultants (Table Games and F&B), develop a capital expenditures budget, review 2003 budget/business plan, labor costs and develop a reorganization plan.

● Page 2

Exhibit 11

Memo

To: Michael Paulson

From: Greg Violette

CC:

Date: January 25, 2003

Re: Wildlife Habitat/Capital Spending

I did some research today on the Wildlife Habitat project – researched a file about three inches thick that Barbara gave me. I pulled out the most pertinent documents and highlighted key information for your convenience (see attachments). They have been working on this project for a couple years, but it seems to have been accelerated in the last couple months.

Wright says $70,000 has been spent to date, and Duff Taylor was about to make a serious commitment for considerable additional funding. I'm not sure if, or how, Larry Nisbet is being compensated, but he will be in the office next week, and I will find out. Wright Wilson claims ignorance. As I mentioned in our last phone conversation, Larry has occupied the office next to Barbara's since I was last there, and there is a sign on the door with his name and the title "Lost City Project Coordinator".

This is only one symptom of a much bigger problem – spending that is out of control and no capital expenditures budget, cash management, or cash forecasting. I have not seen any cohesive planning for capital expenditures. Other significant capital projects have come to light in the last couple days, where significant funds have either been spent or committed. I will provide you with the details as I receive them.

There needs to be a capital spending plan, where projects and their estimated costs are detailed, and then they should be prioritized. The return on investment and payback period should be estimated on those projects where there is a return that can be quantified. I am making it a priority to develop this plan next week, with involvement of key staff members.

1

Before we embark on any elaborate projects or commit any funds to expenditures that do not have an immediate return, we need to get our house in order – get the right management in place, develop a vision and do some strategic planning. I'm concerned that we are trying to be all things to all people. We need to determine what our market niche is, and maximize our return with that segment. We need to improve and refine the product that we already have before we change it. We have to get back to the basics – learn how to walk properly before we try running.

With that in mind, I will be canceling commitments, where I can, for projects that are unnecessary, high risk and/or expensive, and just saying "no" to others that are being proposed. Of course I will be discussing each one with you as I obtain the details. The Animal Habitat will be the first one that I "put on the shelf".

Duff and Wright also were planning to buy 50 TV's that would have internet access. They signed contracts and committed to an initial investment of $65,000. This does not fit into the market by any stretch of the imagination. That type of thing would work in a market that accommodates business travelers and conventions, not a leisure destination. Do senior citizens really care about checking their email? I was able to postpone, and possible cancel that commitment.

Duff and Wright really screwed up the PDS equipment financing. The original terms were awful, and then choosing not to pay, rather than negotiating new terms, was disastrous. The remedy is going to be very expensive. The $500,000 + payment that was made this week will seriously hinder our ability to fund the capital improvements that need to be made. I'm operating under the assumption that the capital expenditures budget will be no higher than the anticipated cash flow from operations, after debt service.

The "Balloon" is another serious commitment that has been made. It may be too late to retreat on that one. I've also enclosed the proforma for that project. I haven't had time to study it yet, but my initial concern is that it doesn't fit with the market (senior citizens). Will it really bring incremental business to the property? I'm keeping an open mind until I discuss it with you further.

RIVER PALMS
Operational Assessment

POSITIVES

CURB APPEAL
CLEAN
GOOD REPORTING SYSTEMS
SLOT FLOOR
PLAYER TRACKING
BINGO

NEGATIVES

PROFITABLILITY FAR BELOW POTENTIAL
MORALITY ISSUES
ETHICS ISSUES
MISCONDUCT
MISMANAGEMENT
IRRESPONSIBLE & WASTEFUL SPENDING
POOR SUPERVISION
NO ACCOUNTABILITY
NO DISCIPLINE
LOW PERFORMANCE STANDARDS
LOW EXPECTATIONS
POOR WORK ETHIC
POOR ATTITUDES
LOW MORALE
HIGH TURNOVER
RAMPANT FAVORITISM
INCONSISTENT TREATMENT OF EMPLOYEES
COMP POLICY ABUSE
LOW REGARD FOR HOURLY EMPLOYEES

Exhibit 13

STRATEGIC TURNAROUND PLAN

A) STOP THE BLEEDING
    1) Cancel/Defer Three Capital Projects
    2) Terminate Five Consulting Agreements
    3) Terminate Lease Agreement for Limousine
    4) Eliminate/Limit the Use of Cell Phones
    5) Cancel Rapid Roulette
    6) Reduce Participation Games
    7) Cancel Unnecessary Newspaper & Magazine subscriptions
    8) Eliminate daily delivery of Coffee & Doughnuts to all work stations
    9) Revise the Comp Policy
        a) Tighten controls over guest comps
        b) Limit the number of managers authorized to comp themselves
        c) Eliminate liquor comps
        d) Require all managers to eat in the EDR at least 3 days a week

B) FINALIZE THE 2003 BUDGETS

C) PREPARE A CAPITAL SPENDING PLAN

D) STAFFING REORGANIZATION

E) CULTURE CHANGE (the way we operate the business)

    1) Maintain the highest ethical and moral standards
    2) Integrity
    3) Professionalism
    4) Honesty
    5) Fairness
    6) Honor the hourly employees
        a) Improve job satisfaction
        b) Improve morale
        c) New internal Company Slogan – "Take Good Care of our Guests and the People Who Serve Them"

F) DEPARTMENT LEVEL MISSION & GOAL SETTING, EFFICIENCY REVIEW

G) BASIC MANAGEMENT & SUPERVISORY TRAINING

H) IMPROVE PRODUCTIVITY W/ BETTER SCHEDULING & LESS OVERTIME

I) REDUCE OPERATING EXPENSES WITH MORE FOCUS & BETTER PURCHASING CONTROLS

Exhibit 14

Page 1 of 2

greg violette

From:	"greg violette" <gviovegas@lvcm.com>
To:	"Michael Paulson" <JMICHAELPA@aol.com>
Sent:	Saturday, February 01, 2003 5:00 PM
Attach:	STRATEGIC TURNAROUND PLAN.doc
Subject:	Weekly Activity Report

Mike,

The most important thing I've accomplished to date, which is also the first step in my Strategic Plan, was to STOP THE BLEEDING. That was done with the following actions:

1) Get Duff Taylor off property, since he was the primary source of irresponsible and wasteful spending.

2) Cancelled/deferred three capital spending projects - Animal Habitat, Balloon, and 50 PC/TV's.

3) Terminated Consulting Agreements (Pat Cruzen, George Maragos, Carl Wolfbrandt, and Larry Nisbet). Mike Algeier (Table Games) will be terminated within two weeks. Mark Bryant and Don Wiggington remain as part time computer specialists, maintaining and enhancing current systems, but I would consider them vendors, rather than consultants.

4) Terminated lease agreement for Limousine.

5) Cancelled two cell phones used by non-employees.

6) Revised the Comp Policy. The Staff has agreed to the following changes:
    A) Tighten controls over guest comps. Ensure that they
        have enough "play" to qualify for a comp, and that
        the comp they are given is commensurate with their
        level of play.
    B) Reduce the number of employees authorized to
        comp themselves for meals.
    C) Eliminate comps for liquor
    D) Require all managers and executives to eat in the
        Employee Dining Room at least three days a week.

The new policy will be issued within two weeks. All of these changes were volunteered by the people who will be affected the most. They knew it was the right thing to do.

The most positive accomplishment to date came at an Executive Staff Meeting on Thursday, where I outlined my Strategic Plan (Turnaround Plan) - see Attachment. It was very well received. The VP's were obviously being led down the wrong path, and they all knew it. They were starving for someone to give them the proper direction, and are excited about following me down the right road.

The most important part of my Strategic Plan, is the Reorganization, where I hope to eliminate 5% of the total workforce, and realize at least $1 million in annual labor savings. The lay-offs will come from all levels of the organization - from VP's down to hourly workers. The VP's will participate. Each of them will submit a plan next week for Wright and I to review. It will involve eliminating positions, consolidating positions, and realigning responsibilities. We hope to make these cuts, which I am calling Phase One, within two weeks. They will not impact revenue or Customer Service. We are just getting rid of the "fat". We will be continuing this process (fine tuning) in the coming weeks and months.

They were also very receptive to my proposal for a major change in the corporate "culture" - the guiding principles that we use to operate the business.

I met with Bob Bilbray, as we discussed last night. I will talk to him again, to see if there is any hope for a

2/17/2003

45

settlement.

I have spent considerable time with Joe Dorsey assisting him in his investigation. He has spent his entire career in security/law enforcement, and he has never seen so much abuse by one man. He has built a strong case, and will present it to you near the end of next week.

I have also begun soliciting ideas from employees and customers on how to improve the business. I am keeping a list, and will implement some suggested changes after reviewing them with Staff.

Looking forward to your visit next week.

Greg

2/17/2003

STEP TWO – REORGANIZATION & WORKFORCE REDUCTION

"A few of these people can drag down the morale of an entire company. I call it cancer, because it can eat away at a company, and spread if not contained. "

In my first week I started this process by emphasizing to the executive staff the importance of improving efficiency and reducing costs. I asked them to meet with their managers and come up with a plan for labor cost reduction.

I asked the HR Director to set up meetings, and over a two week period, she and I and Wright Wilson met with every director and manager to review their staffing and labor reduction plans. Surprisingly, nearly every department volunteered staffing cuts. I asked every manager to justify their staffing levels, and if I didn't think they were offering enough, I would ask some probing questions, and we did some negotiating.

All of the managers that were affected agreed to all of the staffing cuts and changes. It was a voluntary effort. I didn't dictate any changes. This was the first round. I knew there would be more opportunities identified after the introduction of Demand Scheduling.

These Staffing meetings also allowed me to evaluate talent. I got to know every manager and director as well as I could in a two week period. I was able to identify the good and bad managers, those with potential for advancement and those without.

It was obvious that the organization was top heavy, and I really wanted to fire all the vice presidents, but I had to keep Wright Wilson for continuity, and he convinced me to keep his buddy Dean Bridge. All of the other VP's were either fired or demoted. I retained Rose Thompson (Human Resources) only until the reorganization was completed.

I discussed all of my recommended changes in the management ranks with Wright and Rose. I had to consider their opinion of these people, since they knew them much better than me. In almost every case my impressions and judgements about people were right on the money. I didn't have any problem convincing them that these changes were necessary.

Because I was a consultant and didn't have the authority to hire and fire, Wright and Rose had to do the management terminations, demotions and pay reductions - lucky me. I'm sure it was difficult for them, because they were firing their peers, knowing they were just as guilty as them.

I don't like firing people. It's a traumatic experience for the employee. They go through the same grieving and recovery process as they would if there were a death in the family. I've been there. So I take pride in knowing that I've only had to fire a handful of people in my career. I get much more satisfaction out of turning around a problem employee than terminating them. However, this was a turnaround. I had to take a different approach. Rehabilitation was not part of my plan.

I have a lot of empathy for these people. I try to cushion the blow as much as I can. Terminations are part of the job, but I don't take the responsibility lightly.

During my investigation and staffing meetings, a number of employees were identified in different conversations as being trouble makers. You know what I'm talking about. Every company has them - people with negative attitudes, unhappy people that like to make life miserable for others. A few of these people can drag down the morale of an entire company. I call it cancer, because it can eat away at a company, and spread if not contained.

In meetings with the executive staff I told them it was my mission to eradicate the cancer – get rid of all the bad people. There are some people I don't mind firing. But it's frustrating when you find that some of these people have been with the company for a long time, and don't have any reprimands in their file. The failure to document disciplinary issues is a big problem. That makes it difficult to get rid of people. It's part of the lack of accountability that was rampant at the River Palms, and is usually a symptom of a dysfunctional company.

We were able to get rid of most of the "bad apples". This is a really important part of a turnaround project. It speaks to the mental health of the company. The physical health of the company is easier to fix.

I should note that it's not always that easy to terminate employees. I consulted with the company's attorney regarding my plans, and got his approval to proceed before taking action. We were lucky not to have any unions to deal with, and all of the layoffs were due to "downsizing" and "reorganization". Nobody was terminated for "cause", and everybody got their unemployment.

A side benefit of this process of improving labor productivity is that you identify weaknesses in the organizational structure, just by talking to people and asking questions. This usually means a manager is reporting to the wrong person. It can cause inefficiency and affect customer service. I identified many of these weaknesses and corrected them as part of the Reorganization.

The highlights of the Reorganization Plan, summarized above, are detailed in my third Weekly Report (Exhibit 15). My plans for the next phase of the turnaround are announced in my Activity Report for Week Four (Exhibit 16).

Michael called to inform me of Duff Taylor's "resignation". I wrote a press release for Michael to announce the reorganization (Exhibit 17). I also wrote a memo from him to "All Employees" on the same topic (Exhibit 18).

After the layoffs and organizational changes were announced, I thought it was important for me to speak directly to the employees. Wright and I developed a presentation that we gave to all supervisors, managers and salaried employees (more than 200), in groups, over a three day period. I explained the reasons for the changes, how the company would now be operated and reasons why they should be optimistic about the future (Exhibit 19).

I also identified the areas that I believed had the most opportunity to make a significant impact on the company (Exhibit 20).

Exhibit 21 is a list of the changes I made in top management.

Two complimentary letters that I received from employees are displayed in Exhibits 22 and 23. Actually, they were sent to Michael Paulson, which is even better. I knew I was making a positive impact, but it's always nice to hear it. It gave me additional motivation to keep forging ahead. I still had the pedal to the metal after one month, and wasn't about to slow down.

Exhibit 15

Page 1 of 1

greg violette

From:	"greg violette" <gviovegas@lvcm.com>
To:	"Michael Paulson" <JMICHAELPA@aol.com>
Sent:	Monday, February 10, 2003 9:38 AM
Subject:	Activity Report

Mike,

As I discussed with you on Friday, we (Wright & Rose) spent all of last week working on a Reorganization Plan and Implementation Plan. The Plan is primarily that which was submitted by the VP's, with some modifications.

Here are the highlights of the Plan:
1) 45 people (4% of the work force) will be laid off. This eliminates most of the fat in the organization, and results in annual savings of more than $1.5 million.
2) Some of the cuts will be due to closing the Pasta Cucina for lunch (it is doing very well for dinner), and closing the Cafe on graveyard. However, that will be offset by opening the Buffet on graveyard. This is already happening on Tuesdays, but we will expand it to seven days a week.
3) The three highest ranking executives to be terminated are the F&B Director, Surveillance Director and Table Games Director (actually a consultant who, for all intents and purposes, has been running the department). They all have capable assistants who will be promoted.
4) There will be no more VP's. There will be eight directors over the following areas: Finance, Human Resources, Marketing, Surveillance, Hotel Operations, F&B, Gaming and Facilities.
5) Structural changes will be made to achieve optimal utilization of the existing talent. John Strickland will be Director of Hotel Operations, which will include Reservations, which has been reporting to Marketing and he will also be responsible for Housekeeping, which has been reporting to Facilities. He will also supervise the Sales Department. George Yuill gives up Housekeeping, but takes on Security (George has a background in law enforcement). The Banquets Department will be strengthened by promoting a lady who has been working in Special Events, and will report to the F&B Director. Dean Bridge will be responsible for Slots, Table Games, and Bingo. George Yuill and John Strickland will have their pay reduced to the $70,000 to $80,000 range. The Security Director will be demoted to a Shift Manager, and the Beverage Manager will be demoted to Special Events Beverage Manager, both with pay cuts.

The detailed plan was given to you on Friday. You also received the Implementation Plan, which is still being fine-tuned, but is being carefully thought out. We have consulted with counsel to minimze the legal impact.

The overall Turnaround Plan is well under way, and you were also given a copy of that on Friday.

Will give further analysis to elimination of Rapid Roulette and reduction of the participation games. Will consult with you before any action is taken.

Greg

2/17/2003

51

GREG VIOLETTE CONSULTING

Memo

To: MICHAEL PAULSON

From: GREG VIOLETTE

Date: February 18, 2003

Re: ACTIVITY REPORT (2/10-2/14)

Layoffs and management restructuring were completed on Thursday. A total of 26 employees were laid off, and eight other open positions were eliminated. Six more employees will be laid off next Wednesday, with the closing of the Café on the graveyard shift, which will bring the total of positions eliminated to 40. In addition, the duties and responsibilities of many management positions were restructured, titles changed, etc. There are no more VP's. You were given a list of the directors and their direct reports. The organization charts will be distributed next week.

The last two days were primarily devoted to motivational meetings with employees and correspondence to communicate the changes. I also did some work on the re-financing of the existing debt.

The third and final phase of the turnaround will begin next week. That will include implementing the culture change, training and development of management, improving morale, and continuing the efforts to improve efficiency and productivity. This next phase is just as important as the reorganization. "Take good care of our customers......and the people who serve them" will be our internal motto. Focus will be on communicating expectations, raising performance standards, and improving accountability. The 2003 Budget, Capital Plan and new Comp Policy will also be finalized next week.

1

Exhibit 17

For Immediate Release

River Palms Announces New Changes

(Laughlin, NV) In an effort to increase efficiency and productivity, while attaining maximum utilization of the skills and experience of its management team, the River Palms Resort and Casino has announced a restructuring of its organization. In addition to a realignment of management responsibilities, the total workforce was reduced by about 3%, which included about 34 salaried and hourly employees, plus the elimination of 8 positions that were vacant.

Also, Duff Taylor, the General Manager of the River Palms since December 1999, announced his resignation this week to pursue other endeavors. According to Michael Paulson, President and Acting General Manager, "We appreciate Duff Taylor's three years of service at the River Palms, and wish him well in his future endeavors. Our reorganization of the River Palms was designed to streamline the operations and position us to better meet market conditions and respond to the needs of our customers."

The department heads resulting from the reorganization are as follows:

Director of Finance - Wright Wilson
Director of Gaming - Dean Bridge
Director of Sales & Hotel Operations - John Strickland
Director of Food & Beverage - John Maskovich
Director of Marketing - Janette Hallmark
Director of Security & Surveillance - Mike Wright
Director of Human Resources - Rose Thompson
Director of Facilities - George Yuill

The River Palms Resort & Casino features over 1,000 guest rooms & suites, 71,300 square feet of gaming space, 7 restaurants and five lounges, 22,000 square feet of meeting and convention space, hand car wash, retail outlets, hair salon, health spa and a premium beach facility. For additional information visit the River Palms web site at www.rvrpalm.com.

For more information contact:
Robert DeLaRosa

Exhibit 18

**RIVER PALMS
RESORT * CASINO**

Memo

To: ALL EMPLOYEES

From: MICHAEL PAULSON

Date: February 19, 2003

Re: CHANGES

Duff Taylor has resigned from his position as the General Manager to pursue other endeavors. I appreciate his efforts during his three years of service at the River Palms, and wish him well in his future endeavors.

Many needed changes have taken place in the last thirty days. We are reevaluating the whole operations, including various capital projects, and will take actions designed to eliminate unnecessary spending. The Comp Policy is being revised, and a capital spending plan is being finalized. In an effort to improve efficiency and productivity, and attain maximum utilization of the skills and experience of the existing personnel, the management was restructured and unnecessary positions were eliminated.

In this endeavor, the new list of Directors, and their responsibilities, has already been communicated to you. Also, Pasta Cucina will now be open for dinner only. As well, the Café will be closed on the graveyard shift, and have opened the Buffet at that time, with the intent of improving the efficiency of our late night dining service.

All of these changes will result in a substantial increase in efficiency, with little impact on servicing our customers. We will continue to streamline the operations, with a new focus on improving management, taking better care of the customers and the employees who serve them. Many of you will be consulted in the near future, soliciting your input and ideas on ways to improve the operation and job satisfaction.

Until further notice, I will continue to act as the General Manager. Wright Wilson will continue to serve as Assistant General Manager/CFO and oversee the day-to-day operations of the business. Greg Violette, will continue to consult with the management staff in directing the efforts to implement the changes noted above.

We believe these changes will have a positive impact on the River Palms, on you as individuals and the organization as a whole. Thank you for your hard work, team effort and dedication to make the River Palms the best it can be.

1

Exhibit 19

Page 1 of 1

greg violette

From: "greg violette" <gviovegas@lvcm.com>
To: "Michael Paulson" <JMICHAELPA@aol.com>
Sent: Sunday, February 23, 2003 9:20 PM
Subject: Activity Report - Week of 2/17

Mike,

Wright and I conducted our third "Revival" Meeting with about 75 front line supervisors - communicating the reasons for the changes, exactly what we have done, and plans for the future.

Spent a lot of time this week planning and starting the implementation of the final phase of the turnaround, which will include departmental team meetings to establish goals and objectives, improve efficiency and job satisfaction; focus groups with hourly employees to receive their input on suggested changes to improve the operation and increase job satisfaction; and management training. I have developed a one hour training class for everyone who has supervisory responsibilities. I call it Common Sense Management. It is the philosophy I have developed over the past 25 years of managing people. I will be personally conducting this class in groups of 15 over the next four to six weeks.

I now have a River Palms email address, and will be sending that to you on Monday. I will also send you a package next week, which includes the final details of the Reorganization, updated Strategic Turnaround Plan, final revised Comp Policy, etc.

Below is a listing of my day to day activities for the week of February 17:

2/17 - Comp Policy Revision
    Barbara Alacantara email research
    Activity Report for prior week
    Turnaround - Phase III planning

2/18 - Comp Policy Revision
    Debra Bell (craps dealer) complaint research
    Meeting with Security & Surveillance departments
    Finalize Reorganization Detail Report
    Planning session with Wright & Rose

2/19 - Directors' Meeting - communicate Phase III plan
    "Revival" Meeting with front line supervisors

2/20 - Meeting with Players Club & Marketing management
        team to resolve complaint from Club Manager
    Meeting with Debra Bell and Table Games mgmt
    Develop Management Training Program

2/21 - Marketing Meeting
    Meeting with Kent Merker of Bridge Capital
        regarding refinancing
    Directors Meeting -conducted mgmt training class

2/22 - Meeting with Bill Strachan of Yellowstone Mgmt   regarding refinancing

Take care,
Greg

2/23/2003

55

Exhibit 20

RIVER PALMS RESORT * CASINO
Opportunities

POKER

GROUP SALES

ROOM SERVICE

PLAYER DEVELOPMENT

BLUES FESTIVAL

ARRIVAL EXPERIENCE

SUN COUNTRY AIRLINES

F&B PRODUCTIVITY

LASER LIGHT SHOW

TABLE GAMES

RIVER PALMS RESORT * CASINO
Executive Position Changes

General Manager, Duff Taylor, terminated 2/15

Michael Paulson, appointed himself to Acting General Manager 2/15

Wright Wilson, Vice President & CFO appointed to CFO & Acting Assistant General Manager 2/15

Director of Surveillance, Fred Sayre, terminated 2/11

Director of Food & Beverage, Richard Ross, terminated 2/11

Director of Security, Carl Tese, demoted 2/12, terminated 3/28

Director of Security & Surveillance, Mike Wright promoted 2/12, terminated 4/1

Director of Table Games, Mike Algeier, terminated 2/21

Dean Bridge, Vice President of Slot Operations, transferred to Director of Gaming 2/16

Vice President of Hotel Operations & Facilities, George Yuill, Demoted to Director of Facilities 2/16, terminated 3/27

Vice President of Marketing, John Strickland, transferred to Director Of Hotel Operations & Sales 2/16

Vice President of Human Resources, Rose Thompson, terminated 3/27

Exhibit 22

February 25, 2003

Mr. Michael Paulson
Boulder City, NV

REF: River Palms Resort Casino

Dear Mr. Paulson:

My name is Jeanne Patskan. I am the Employee Relations/Benefits Manager for the River Palms Resort Casino. I have worked for River Palms for six years now. I am writing to thank you for stepping in and doing something about the mismanagement that was occurring at the River Palms for so long. I believe that River Palms can be the best hotel/casino on the river with the proper management team in place. Greg Violette has been a breath of fresh air to this property. I cannot stress to you enough, the exceptional job he has done in implementing this reorganization. Mr. Violette has maintained a professionalism, unlike any this property has seen in quite some time. He has also shown a respect and fairness to our single biggest resource, the employee.

In a meeting I recently attended, it was mentioned that "Mr. Violette was here on a temporary basis and would be leaving very soon". This is what compelled me to write this letter. I wish to express my concern if this is truly to take place. As, many of the same key players are still in place and I strongly feel, if Mr. Violette leaves, we will merely go right back to our old ways. We need <u>someone</u> to not only oversee the general operation, but to also protect your assets.

I trust my identity will remain confidential, as I stated above, the same key players are still in place and my job could be jeopardized. I sincerely hope that I have not over stepped my bounds by contacting you personally, however, it's something I feel very strongly about and I would never abuse my ability to have access to the needed information for me to contact you. I am dedicated to the success of the River Palms and hope to work here for many years to come.

Warmest Regards,

Jeanne Patskan
7491 Martin Dr.
Mohave Valley, AZ 86440

Exhibit 23

2/26/03

DEAR MR. PAULSON,

PLEASE ALLOW ME TO REINTRODUCE MYSELF TO YOU. WE FIRST MET AT THE
RIVER PALMS MANAGEMENT PICNIC BACK IN 2001. MY NAME IS JULIE MOODY
AND I AM YOUR PAYROLL MANAGER AT RIVER PALMS. I HAVE THE MOST
SENIORITY OF ANYONE ON PROPERTY (ALMOST 18 1/2 YEARS) SO YOU CAN
IMAGINE ALL THE COMINGS AND GOINGS I HAVE WITNESSED. AFTER ALL
THESE YEARS, YOU WOULD THINK NOTHING SHOULD SURPRISE ME ANYMORE.
HOWEVER, I AM STILL AMAZED AT THE SHENANIGANS "KEY" PERSONNEL PULL
WHEN THEY THINK THEY DON'T HAVE TO ACCOUNT TO ANYONE FOR THEIR
ACTIONS INCLUDING THE MANAGEMENT GROUP THAT HAS BEEN IN PLACE FOR
APPROXIMATELY THE LAST 2 1/2 YEARS OR SO.

THAT BEING SAID, I'D LIKE TO PERSONALLY **THANK YOU** FOR SENDING MR.
GREG VIOLETTE TO OUR RESCUE! THAT IS HOW MANY OF US FEEL THAT HAVE
BEEN WITH THE PROPERTY FOR A NUMBER OF YEARS - WE ARE BEING RESCUED.
HIS PRESENCE ON PROPERTY HAS PUT AN END TO MANY OF THE COMP ABUSES
AND THE UNWARRANTABLE "PERCS" KEY PERSONNEL AND THEIR FEW SELECT
"BUDDIES" WERE ENJOYING FOR FAR TOO LONG. WE HAVE BEEN LED TO BELIEVE
THAT YOU HAD NO INTEREST IN US DOWN HERE IN LAUGHLIN - THAT YOU WOULD
JUST AS SOON "DUMP" THE PROPERTY AS TO HAVE TO DEAL WITH US. I BELIEVE
YOUR SEEMINGLY INATTENTION TO US GAVE THE MANAGEMENT TEAM A FALSE
SENSE OF SECURITY. THEY THOUGHT THEY COULD GET AWAY WITH THINGS (AND
THEY DID) BECAUSE YOU DID NOT MAKE YOUR PRESENCE KNOWN ON PROPERTY
AS OFTEN AS SOME OF US WOULD HAVE LIKED TO HAVE SEEN.

YOU CERTAINLY SURPRISED EVERYONE BY SENDING GREG TO OUR PROPERTY.
HIS PRESENCE WAS LONG OVERDUE. THE POSITIVE CHANGES HE HAS MADE, IN
A VERY SHORT TIME, ARE COMMENDABLE. HIS NAME BADGE SAYS HE IS THE
"OWNER'S REPRESENTATIVE" AND HE DOES AN EXCELLENT JOB OF REPRESENTING
YOU, MR. PAULSON. HIS DEMEANOR IS VERY PROFESSIONAL. HE DOES NOT
HAVE A FOLLOWING OF "BUDDIES" ON PROPERTY SO HE MAKES DECISIONS THAT
ARE FAIR, THAT ARE THE RIGHT THINGS TO DO AND IN <u>YOUR</u> BEST INTERESTS.
HE MINGLES WITH THE HOURLY EMPLOYEES AND SITS IN THE EMPLOYEE DINING
ROOM AND ACTUALLY TALKS WITH THEM. HE GIVES THEM THE OPPORTUNITY
TO EXPRESS THEIR OPINIONS ON THINGS THAT MATTER TO THEM. WE ARE
CONDUCTING BUSINESS IN A POSITIVE NEW WAY AT THE RIVER PALMS - ALL
BECAUSE YOU <u>DO</u> CARE!

I BELIEVE YOU WOULD HAVE BEEN VERY PROUD OF THE WAY HE REPRESENTED
YOU AT THE MANAGERS MEETING HELD ON 2/13. HE GOT UP IN FRONT OF THE
GROUP AND TOLD US EXACTLY HOW BAD THINGS HAD BEEN RUNNING. HE DID NOT
"SUGAR COAT" ANY OF HIS WORDS. HE TOLD IT LIKE IT NEEDED TO BE SAID
FOR A VERY LONG TIME NOW. I HARDLY KNOW THIS MAN AND I WAS DARN PROUD
OF HIM! IT WOULD BE MY FERVENT HOPE THAT YOU ARE PLANNING ON KEEPING
GREG AT THE RIVER PALMS FOR A LONG TIME. HE HAS MADE SUCH AN IMPACT
IN SUCH A BRIEF TIME, IMAGINE WHAT HE COULD DO FOR THE PROPERTY LONG
TERM.

THERE MAY BE SOME RESENTMENT AMONG SOME "KEY" EMPLOYEES OF GREG'S
PRESENCE ON PROPERTY. THIS IS BECAUSE THEY HAVE NEVER BEEN HELD
ACCOUNTABLE FOR THEIR ACTIONS OR DECISION AND THEY DON'T WANT TO
START ANSWERING TO AN "OWNER'S REPRESENTATIVE" NOW. IT IS MY
OPINION THAT IF GREG WERE NOT ON PROPERTY, THAT DECISIONS WOULD BE
MADE THAT WOULD NOT NECESSARILY BE IN YOUR BEST INTERESTS. THE
"SHENANIGANS" WOULD START UP AGAIN IF THEY KNEW THEY DID NOT HAVE
TO ACCOUNT TO ANYONE.

I WANT OUR CASINO TO BE THE BEST ON THE RIVER AND A VISITOR'S FIRST
CHOICE WHEN COMING TO LAUGHLIN. I ALSO WANT TO BE PROUD TO SAY THAT
I AM PART OF THE RIVER PALMS TEAM AND HAVE A MANAGEMENT TEAM THAT I
CAN LOOK UP TO AS ROLE MODELS, WHO CONDUCT THEMSELVES IN A PROFESSIONAL
MANNER AND WHOSE MORAL BEHAVIOR DOES NOT BRING DISCREDIT TO OUR
PROPERTY. I BELIEVE THAT WITH GREG'S PRESENCE AND GUIDANCE THAT THESE
THINGS WILL BE ATTAINED!

I HOPE THAT MY CORRESPONDENCE TO YOU STAYS CONFIDENTIAL BECAUSE SOME
OF THE SAME PEOPLE WHO WERE IN CHARGE BEFORE ARE STILL "RUNNING" THIS
OPERATION. I HOPE TO SEE YOU ON PROPERTY IN THE NEAR FUTURE!

I KNOW HOW BUSY YOU ARE SO I THANK YOU FOR TAKING THE TIME TO READ THIS!

SINCERELY,

JULIE MOODY

STEP THREE – MANAGEMENT TRAINING

"My favorite thing to do is praise a subordinate in front of my boss."

Most employees don't get enough training for their first supervisory job. And it's often not done correctly. Some employees never get any proper training on how to supervise. Often times when there is an opening for a supervisor, the best "technician" is selected to lead the group. It could be a group that fixes cars, cooks food, deals cards or cleans the floors. Management will take the one from the group who does their job best - the best "technician" - and promote them to supervisor without teaching them how to manage. The method of selection might be okay, but doing and supervising are two completely different things, and a person has to be trained on how to supervise people.

After 30 years of doing it, I have developed a management style that is effective for me. Everybody develops their own style. I'm very much team oriented, and adhere to the old "Management by Objective" philosophy.

The guiding principle in my approach to managing people is to do everything I can to help my subordinates achieve success. My theory is that, as they become successful, I will rise on their shoulders. I do everything I can to support them, and give them all the credit they deserve. I never claimed to be an expert at anything, but I tried to hire experts, and help them succeed.

My philosophy is very basic. I call it "Common Sense Management", because it seems to be just that – common sense. It's not something I learned in school – just came from years of experience. I place a high priority on satisfying the needs of the employee. If an employee's basic needs are met, they will be more productive. If they are happy with their job, they will perform better. All people have different needs, so you have to tailor your supervision to fit the individual.

My philosophy, In a nutshell - hire good, qualified people, train them properly, give them the tools they need and a comfortable, secure work environment. Give them a well-defined job description and set goals and objectives. Ensure that they know what they are responsible for and the authority they have. Give a lot of feedback on a regular basis, so they always know where they stand. Praise in public, counsel in private.

My favorite thing to do is praise a subordinate in front of my boss. "Hey boss, did you notice what a great job that Dennis did on that business plan? He worked really hard on it. I'm proud of him." What a rush that is, when you're the subordinate!

Other topics are included in my class. This is the outline:

1) How to be Successful in your Career

2) Ingredients for Success

3) How to be a Good Employee

4) How to be a Good Manager

5) Qualities of a Good Manager

Exhibit 24 is an outline of the Common Sense Management training program.

Exhibits 25 – 28 are my Activity Reports for my second month on the job, and they include details about the management training initiative and a myriad of other issues that I dealt with while I was doing the training.

Exhibit 29 is a complimentary letter from an employee.

Hold an image of the life you want....
And that image will become FACT

Exhibit 24

COMMON SENSE MANAGEMENT

HOW TO BE SUCCESSFUL IN YOUR CAREER

Have a Vision

Set Goals

Overcome Obstacles

Look and Act the Part

Impress your Boss's Boss

Be a Good Employee

Be a Good Manager

INGREDIENTS FOR SUCCESS

Intelligence

Common Sense

Good Communications Skills

Be a Team Player

Get Along Well with Others

Strong Work Ethic

BE A GOOD EMPLOYEE

GOAL NUMBER ONE – PLEASE YOUR BOSS

Help Him Achieve His Goals

Accomplish Your Objectives

Meet or Exceed Expectations

Accuracy & Timeliness

Be Organized

Be Loyal

HOW TO BE A GOOD MANAGER

GOAL NUMBER TWO – Help your subordinates become successful

SATISFY EMPLOYEE NEEDS
      Detailed Job Description
      Goals
      Objectives
      Priorities
      Expectations
      Well defined authority
      Support
      Tools
      Training
      Working conditions
      Fairness
      Honesty
      Consistency
      Feedback
            Be lavish with your praise – do it in public
            Criticize in private
      Follow the Golden Rule
      Personal Needs

QUALITIES OF A GOOD MANAGER

TEMPERAMENT
HIRE QUALITY PEOPLE
FOLLOW THROUGH ON COMMITMENTS
DELEGATE EFFECTIVELY
SET HIGH STANDARDS
CHALLENGE YOUR SUBORDINATES
CREATE TEAMWORK
BE A GOOD FACILITATOR
BUILD CONSENSUS
RESOLVE CONFLICTS IN A PROFESSIONAL MANNER ON A TIMELY BASIS
KEEP WORKING RELATIONSHIPS PROFESSIONAL
IDENTIFY THE STARS AND NURTURE THEM
BE PROFESSIONAL – TEACH & PRACTICE OFFICE ETIQUETTE
MAKE HUMAN RESOURCES & PAYROLL YOUR BEST FRIENDS
DO YOUR PAPERWORK ACCURATELY AND ON TIME
DO EVALUATIONS & GIVE RAISES ON TIME
MOTIVATION
STRESS IS SELF-INFLICTED

Exhibit 25

Page 1 of 1

Greg Violette

From:	"Greg Violette" <gviovegas@riverpalms.net>
To:	<JMICHAELPA@aol.com>
Sent:	Monday, March 03, 2003 12:22 PM
Subject:	Activity Report - Week Ending March 2

Mike,

I spent considerable time last week preparing the outline for the management training class, which I will start presenting this week. Also spent some time investigating allegations in an anonymous letter, which I have mailed to you, with the final decision being not to pursue any type of formal investigation - the writer is most likely an employee who was laid off.

Discussed payroll issues in a meeting with F&B leadership. This area has been dysfunctional, but we have a game plan and a new focus that I believe will resolve the issues.

Attended an Orientation session and addressed the group. We had a Directors' Meeting, where we got the group to start outlining their own personal goals and objectives. Departmental Efficiency Review Meetings are now under way. Also attended the Employee of the Month Awards Ceremony.

Attended a preview of the Lazer Light Show. I think it has potential, if we can customize it to appeal to our audience. We also had a meeting afterward to discuss how to customize it and market it.

Conducted a meeting with two problem employees (cocktail servers). I believe we have diffused the issue. Cocktail servers and dealers were the most unhappy groups in the company, but I believe the changes we have made in the management of those two groups have turned things around. There seems to be much more harmony and improved morale.

Also spent the better part of an afternoon obtaining a work card and Emergency Access Card that the city is issuing to key employees in case there are problems during the River Run, and access to and from the city is limited.

Greg

3/3/2003

Exhibit 26	Page 1 of 1

greg violette

From: "greg violette" <gviovegas@lvcm.com>
To: "Michael Paulson" <JMICHAELPA@aol.com>
Sent: Sunday, March 09, 2003 8:37 PM
Attach: COMMON SENSE MANAGEMENT.doc
Subject: Activity Report

Mike,

Most of my time this week was spent conducting management training classes. About sixty managers and supervisors have now been through my class, called Common Sense Management. Attached is an outline of the class. In the class I also address the need to improve labor cost management, scheduling, overtime, etc., and the need to improve our orientation for new employees (27% of all employees leave in the first 30 days). The class lasts about three hours. The feedback I have gotten from many who have attended the class is very positive.

I'm continuing the process of establishing goals and objectives for all departments. Held a meeting with F&B management to address labor issues. Met with five beverage servers, who have been identified as "problem" employees.

Facilitated a meeting with Sales, Marketing & F&B managers to assign responsibilities in areas that overlap, specifically busing, convention and banquet sales.

Also met confidentially with the Director of Finance, who had complaints about Wright Wilson.

Many problems solved, many more to conquer. Lots of challenges, but we have a lot of people believing. Important to keep the momentum going. The employees, in general, like what we're doing, but are skeptical, because they've heard it before.

Regards,
Greg

3/16/2003

68

Exhibit 27

Page 1 of 1

Greg Violette

From: "Greg Violette" <gviovegas@riverpalms.net>
To: <JMICHAELPA@aol.com>
Sent: Thursday, March 13, 2003 11:34 AM
Subject: Activity Report - Week of March 10

Mike,

I took some time off this week, because my parents are in town. Specifically, two days - half day last Friday, half day this Monday, and tomorrow (March 14). Two days will be deducted from my invoice for the month, which is being sent separately.

The 2003 budget has been finalized. The mission statement is near completion. The organization charts are near completion. Director level goals and objectives have been completed, but need some fine tuning.

I believe there is another $500,000 in potential annual labor savings. There are three high level positions that can be eliminated at a savings of $200,000. I will discuss those with you, before making any changes. The rest of the savings is in the hourly ranks, and will result from increased productivity. Those savings will come one body at a time, through attrition. My focus this week has been on teaching the directors how to increase productivity and efficiency through demand scheduling, raising performance standards, controlling overtime, etc.

We had a meeting on Monday with a loan broker representing Imperial Bank, which has a strong interest in doing the refinancing we are looking for.

Next week I will complete my management training with three more three-hour sessions. In addition to that, my focus for the next thirty days will be on finalizing director-level and departmental goals and objectives, reducing labor costs in the hourly ranks (without affecting customer service), and taking our message on changing the culture to the hourly ranks.

Greg

Exhibit 28

Greg Violette

From:	"Greg Violette" <gviovegas@riverpalms.net>
To:	<JMICHAELPA@aol.com>
Sent:	Friday, March 21, 2003 3:24 PM
Subject:	Activity Report - Week Ending March 21

Mike,

I conducted three more management training classes this week, and I believe every manager and supervisor (about 110 people) have now received the training. The class included about 60 minutes of basic supervisory skills, about 60 minutes of how to be successful in your career, about 60 minutes on increasing labor productivity through demand scheduling, raising perfomance standards, and eliminating time clock abuse, and 30 minutes on improving the accuracy and timeliness of paperwork involving labor reporting, and orienting new employees properly to reduce turnover (27% of our employees leave in the first 30 days).

I received a term sheet from e Financial Services of Las Vegas for the refinancing we are pursuing. The terms appear to be acceptable. The funding will come from an insurance company. I had some discussions with them. They have asked for a "resume" on the owner, last three years corporate tax returns, 5-year proforma, business plan for the capital improvements, and a new appraisal. I will be working on that next week.

I will also continue fine-tuning the departmental goals and objectives, which are necessary to implement accountability in the organization. I will start looking at departmental scheduling.

Allegations of misconduct have been made by a Surveillance Agent. Human Resources is performing an investigation. I am performing my own informal investigation. I also received other allegations of misconduct (unrelated) from another source, which I will discuss with you in our next phone conversation.

Greg

3/21/2003

Andre van der Velden
Players Club Supervisor
River Palms Casino

March 18, 2003

Greg Violette
Owner Representative
River Palms Casino

Dear Mr. Violette:

I am writing you today to express my appreciation for the positive changes I have witnessed since you joined the River Palms team. I especially enjoyed your "Common Sense Management" training class and feel that you have brought a badly needed breath of fresh air to the River Palms. Poor customer service and low employee morale have been an ongoing problem at the River Palms ever since I started working here. Under your leadership, I have seen tremendous improvements in customer service, as well as increases in efficiency, productivity, and employee morale. I sincerely hope you will become our General Manager and a permanent member of the River Palms team.

Sincerely,

Andre van der Velden

STEP FOUR – CHANGING THE CULTURE

---

*"I then turned the organization chart upside down -
putting the customers and front line employees at the top and
the general manager at the bottom."*

It's hard to define the culture of an organization. What does that word mean in the context of a company? It's not a word that we used in the business world until late in my career. I guess it can be compared to the culture of a nation, which is defined by its values and traditions. I can't think of a better way to define it, but I do know that it is more difficult to change than any other aspect of the turnaround. That's because it involves changing people's attitudes - the way they think and act.

Unlike other aspects of the turnaround, this part was not repairable. The only option I saw was to "blow it up and start over". So I approached this aspect as I would if I was starting my own company. I would instill my values and philosophy in the workforce. Fortunately, they were in direct contradiction to those of the previous management team.

I started with a Mission Statement. I set up a process that allowed all the employees to provide input, suggestions. Then there was a management review process culminating in a final product that was presented for my approval. I liked the final product (Exhibit 30). It was a five sentence statement, but I added a sixth, "To operate the business with the highest level of integrity and professionalism, the highest ethical and moral values, using the principles of honesty, fairness and consistency."

I then turned the organization chart upside down (Exhibit 31), putting the customers and front line employees at the top and the General Manager at the bottom. I started preaching that the front line employees were our most valuable asset, and the job of management was to support them. "If our employees are happy they will provide better customer service. If we have happy customers they will spend more money and tell their friends."

One of the complaints I heard many times was that management was aloof. For example they had all their meals in the steakhouse, so as to avoid all the hourly folks who were eating in the buffet or the employee dining room. I found that disturbing and thought of a way to send a message. During my first week on the job at the end of my first Executive Staff Meeting, I told the group that I was going to buy them lunch. They all looked at me inquisitively, and I'm sure they were thinking, "We don't have to pay for meals here, so where is he taking us?"

I said, "Follow me", as I got up and led all ten of them to the Employee Dining Room. I'm sure most of them had not been in that room in a long time. I wish I could have seen the looks on their faces when they realized where I was taking them, but I was at the front of the group. I did, however, see the shocked faces on the employees that were eating as we entered the room. I stopped and faced all the "VP's" and said, "We're splitting up – everybody at a different table. Mingle with the troops". And they did.

I don't think that stunt went over very well with the executives, but it didn't matter. Most of them were gone in a few weeks. I did get my message across.

I do believe in leading by example. I made it a point to eat in the employee dining room as often as possible. I would sit with groups of dealers, servers, janitors, etc., and I always brought a notebook. I always asked two questions, "How can we better serve the customer?" and "How can I make your job better?" I took a lot of notes!

I spent considerable time in the evenings just walking around the property. Early in my career I remember some management expert espousing a philosophy of "management by wandering around". I found out that it works, especially at times when executives aren't usually around. I caught a few employees doing bad things, but I also caught a lot of employees doing good things. Whenever I did, I would praise them on the spot, and make sure their boss found out.

It didn't take long for word to get out that I was approachable, and employees would stop me to make a complaint or offer a suggestion. Whenever I got a suggestion or question I couldn't answer, I wrote it down along with their name. I made it a point to respond to every one of them – me personally, not my secretary or an assistant. A lot of those suggestions became a part of my list of Job Enrichment Initiatives (Exhibit 32), which all became a reality during my time at the River Palms.

Now was the time to take my message directly to all the troops. I gave a presentation to all employees in four sessions, with groups of about 250 in each session. I started by telling them that Michael Paulson was upset, because he was losing money and people were taking advantage of him. I talked about how we had to "stop the bleeding", how we cut the fat out of the organization, reorganized to improve efficiency and removed the cancers. Every manager had been trained on how to supervise people.

On the big screen I showed them the new Mission Statement, the new Organizational Chart and the Job Enrichments Initiative, as well as some statistics showing labor productivity improvement over the last two months.

I told them that my efforts going forward would be focused on more management training, including demand scheduling, raising performance standards and introducing accountability. I would be emphasizing fairness and consistency in all management training.

I congratulated them on surviving the cuts, assured them that no more were planned, promised that things would be better and thanked them for their patience and understanding during a time of turmoil. These employees had just experienced a drastic change in culture – from one end of the spectrum to the other.

Exhibits 33 and 35 offer more details on the management reorganization and the Employee Forums. Exhibit 34 is a nice note from Michael Paulson.

RIVER PALMS RESORT * CASINO

MISSION STATEMENT

TO ENSURE THAT "EVERYONE'S A WINNER AT THE RIVER PALMS"

TO ENSURE THAT EVERY CUSTOMER HAS A FUN AND ENTERTAINING EXPERIENCE

TO ENSURE THAT OUR EMPLOYEES HAVE FUN AND ARE EXCITED ABOUT THEIR CONTRIBUTION TO THE SUCCESS OF THE RIVER PALMS

TO ENSURE THAT THE OWNERS ARE PROUD OF THE RIVER PALMS AND ENJOY THE BENEFITS OF A PROFITABLE ENTERPRISE

TO ENSURE THAT OUR VENDORS, OUR COMMUNITY AND OUR PEERS FEEL POSITIVE ABOUT THEIR ASSOCIATION WITH THE RIVER PALMS AS AN UPSTANDING CORPORATE CITIZEN

TO OPERATE THE BUSINESS WITH THE HIGHEST LEVEL OF INTEGRITY AND PROFESSIONALISM, THE HIGHEST ETHICAL AND MORAL VALUES, USING THE PRINCIPLES OF HONESTY, FAIRNESS AND CONSISTENCY

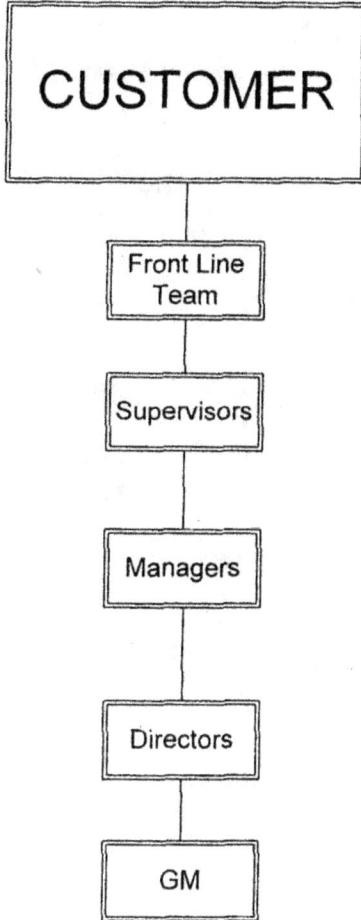

Exhibit 32

RIVER PALMS
Job Enrichment Initiatives

CATCH A STAR PERFORMER PROGRAM (EXISTING)

EMPLOYEE OF THE MONTH/YEAR (EXISTING)

PERFECT ATTENDANCE REWARD PROGRAM

NEW EMPLOYEE INDOCTRINATION

EXPAND BEVERAGE SERVERS' STATION IN BERMUDA CLUB

IMPROVED FOOD QUALITY IN EMPLOYEE DINING ROOM

EMPLOYEE SUGGESTION PROGRAM

OPEN DOOR POLICY

INVITE SELECTED MANAGERS TO EXECUTIVE COMMITTEE MEETINGS

RIVER WALK EMPLOYEE PICNICS SERVED BY MANAGEMENT

EXECUTIVE INTERACTION

EMPLOYEE APPRECIATION DAY

EMPLOYEE BLACKJACK TOURNAMENT

EMPLOYEE RIVER CRUISES

EMPLOYEE TALENT SHOW

EMPLOYEE SLOT TOURNAMENT

HAUNTED HOUSE

CHILI COOK-OFF/EMPLOYEE OLYMPICS

CHRISTMAS PARTY

Exhibit 33

greg violette

From:	"greg violette" <gviovegas@lvcm.com>
To:	"Michael Paulson" <JMICHAELPA@aol.com>
Sent:	Saturday, March 29, 2003 4:44 PM
Subject:	Activity Report - Week of March 24

Mike,

It was a difficult week, with the terminations of Rose Thompson, Director of HR (former VP), George Yuill, Director of Facilities (former VP of Hotel Operations), Carl Tese, Security Supervisor (former Director of Security), and Joe Baird, Surveillance Agent. The first two were eliminating more fat in the organization, and the last two were cancers that had to be removed. None of them will be replaced, except possibly Joe in Surveillance. I wrote letters of recommendation for Rose and George. Since I have had the opportunity to work with them, I realized they both had some good qualities, and a high level of dedication. They were just victims of circumstances - Duff Taylor allowing the organization to get bloated.

Of the original nine VP's and Directors that reported to Duff Taylor, only Wright Wilson, Dean Bridge and John Strickland remain. John is a question mark, for health reasons. We are searching for a replacement for him. You know my concerns about Wright and Dean.

The Surveillance Department "revolt" consumed a lot of time. We met with all the agents Friday morning, and they would not accept the retention of Mike Wright. The degree of their passion caught us off guard, so we had no choice, but to temporarily remove Mike from his responsibility for Surveillance, and ask him to focus only on Security. At a minimum, there needs to be a "cooling off" period. I will discuss a solution with you on Monday.

I had more discussions with e Financial Services, and provided them with more documentation, regarding the refinancing we are seeking. Wright went to Las Vegas last week to discuss the financing with other potential sources.

We had a meeting on Thursday with representatives of Sun Country Airlines. They have asked us to buy blocks of seats on all their flights. We got burned in the past when we did this, and I don't think we can take the risk.

I am continuing my effort to get "the message" to all hourly employees in meetings called Employee Forums. My message is a thirty minute speech outlining 1) How bad it was, 2) The need to change, 3) Improvements we have made, 4) The need to increase productivity with better scheduling and controlling overtime, 5) Raising standards, 6) Establishing accountability, 7) Changing the culture, 8) Improving job satisfaction and 9) the potential we have for further improvement. I am getting tremendous positive feedback from the hourly employees, since most of the problems were with management and they were well aware of what needed to be done. They are extremely pleased that action is finally being taken.

I had the first meeting last week with Housekeeping (50), because it is a one-shift operation, and they have a monthly meeting. I met with all the beverage servers (35) this week in two groups, because they are the most dysfunctional department. Next week I'm meeting with Engineering and Pit Employees in four meetings, because they are also dysfunctional departments. The following week I will meet with the remaining 800 hourly employees in four meetings. I don't think meetings like this have ever been held. They are all given an opportunity to comment at the end of my speech. Wright Wilson also addresses each group. I can sense his discomfort and some resentment from the groups, because he, and they, know that he was a part of the problem.

I attended Employee of the Month and Star Employee awards ceremonies.

Next week I will begin implementation of new controls over other operating expenses, besides labor. This will intensify my efforts to eliminate irresponsible and wasteful spending.

Look forward to your visit on Monday,
Greg

3/29/2003

Exhibit 34

Page 1 of 1

greg violette

From: <JMICHAELPA@aol.com>
To: <gviovegas@lvcrn.com>
Sent: Monday, March 31, 2003 11:48 AM
Subject: Re: Activity Report - Week of March 24

GREG, THOUGH IT WAS A TOUGH WEEK ON A PERSONAL LEVEL, IT SOUNDS LIKE A VERY
PRODUCTIVE WEEK FOR THE RIVER PALMS. GOOD WORK! AND THANK YOU FOR YOUR

DILIGENCE IN MAKING THE RIVER PALMS MORE PRODUCTIVE FOR THE EMPLOYEES AND THE
OWNERS. I WILL CALL YOU LATER AS I WILL NOT BE ABLE TO MAKE IT DOWN TODAY.
BEST REGARDS, MIKE

Exhibit 35

From:	"greg violette" <gviovegas@lvcm.com>
To:	"Michael Paulson" <JMICHAELPA@aol.com>
Sent:	Saturday, April 12, 2003 7:13 PM
Subject:	Activity Report - Week of April 7

Mike,

I gave 30 minute speeches (and Wright added about 20 minutes) to about 900 hourly employees in four groups. The theme was "The Need to Change". I outlined all the things that were wrong with the organization (because they deserved to know the truth; and because if I'm asking them to change, they need to understand why), all the changes we have made, and plans for the future. I emphasized the positive things about the changes - they are now working for a profitable company, and management is focusing on the right things, solving problems, and taking them down the right path (for the first time in many years).

The response has been very positive. People have told me that they have a new sense of comfort knowing they finally have good leadership.

The Manager of Player Development has been terminated, and will not be replaced. She was a cancer in the organization. We contemplated laying her off last month, but thought that she might change - she did not. People with negative attitudes and poor work ethic usually don't change.

The Surveillance Technician also was terminated - he's the guy who moves, fixes, and maintain cameras and related equipment. He was overpaid, had poor performance, and a bad attitude. He will be replaced at a lower salary.

A banquet captain and a banquet server were both terminated. They were cancers. One of them will be replaced.

We are planning to terminate three people from Engineering - the secretary who is unecessary, and two engineers who are also cancers. We will decide for sure on Monday, after consulting again with the top two guys in the Department.

The total number of positions eliminated has now exceeded 50. I assure you they all have had a positive impact on the organization. The work is still getting done, and the morale is much improved. The cancers in the organization were allowed to remain, because of a lack of accountability - management chose not to confront difficult issues. All of the recent terminations have been done either at the urging of, or concurrence with, the Department Managers, Wright Wilson and the HR Manager.

We are now in the fine-tuning stages of the turnaround. We will continue to increase productivity and reduce labor costs, with a new focus on demand scheduling and reducing overtime. I don't expect to make too many more lay-offs, if any. Any terminations from now on will be due to poor performance, and productivity will increased by not replacing people that quit.

I will be doing a lot of teaching and coaching - developing the new managers and directors. Let me remind you that I have accomplished this turnaround without bringing in one person from "the outside".

There is one exception to that - we have hired the Poker Manager from the Riverside (after he quit there). The department needs a "jump start", and the current manager, who is a dealer that was recently promoted and has no management experience, is not capable of doing the things that need to be done. He starts May 5th.

The March financials have been distributed. They look very good - record revenues and profits. I hope to review them with you on Monday. I will also show you the plans to increase table games revenues. I think city-wide revenues may be off in April, due to the war and gas prices. However, I expect our cost reduction efforts to pay dividends, even if the revenues are down.

Hope to see you on Monday,

4/12/2003

STEP FIVE – TEACHING AND COACHING

"You need to take care of your stars – nurture them, make sure they're challenged and adequately compensated."

After two months on the job I realized that all phases of the Turnaround Plan had been implemented. I was pleasantly surprised – thought it would take longer. The time it takes to perform a turnaround is dependent on three things:

1)   Size of the operation

2)   Extent of union involvement

3)   Ability to focus on the turnaround (not involved in daily operations)

I was fortunate in this case to have those factors in my favor.

Even though the plan had been implemented, the turnaround was not complete. There was still a lot of work left, and I had no intention of slowing down. I was going under the assumption that Michael wanted it done as quickly as possible.

I'm sure you've gone to at least one seminar in your life or a training session for your job. How long did it take you to forget the subject matter? If you used that information on a daily basis, incorporated into your job, you will never forget it. If you seldom or never use the information, you will forget it in a matter of days. You may leave a seminar gung-ho about making a change in your life or your job. A few days later it's forgotten, because the change wasn't reinforced.

Learning is a process that takes repetition, reinforcement. That was my objective for the final phase of the turnaround. I wanted my business philosophy and management philosophy instilled in all levels of the organization. I could preach until I'm blue in the face, but my philosophy would not be engrained until I made it a part of their daily routine.

In order to ensure that my policies, as presented to the executive staff, were being communicated and implemented at all levels of the organization, I started attending departmental meetings and interacting with department managers and supervisors. I was able to determine whether my policies and directives were being implemented. I was able to clarify things that could have caused problems, because my intentions were misinterpreted or miscommunicated. It was also a way to hold the Directors accountable. They knew that if I wanted a policy or procedure implemented, I was going to confirm that it was.

The layoffs and organizational changes that I made were kind of like a "first pass". Most of the layoffs were volunteered, with a little prodding. There were still a lot of opportunities for improvement. In some areas I had only scratched the surface. In this last phase of the plan, I dug deeper, identified more problems and fixed more problems.

Actually, I didn't really fix problems myself. I would form groups of people, and ask them to come up with a solution, getting involved only to the extent necessary. Or I would bring up an issue or problem at a staff meeting, and the group would find a solution. In those situations I play the role of "consensus builder". I'm a huge proponent of team building and participative management. When making decisions, I like to solicit input from the people affected.

In the first sixty days I had to make judgments about people with limited information. I think my success rate was pretty high, but not 100%. A couple people got promoted then fired, and a

83

couple got demoted then fired. So there was a continuing process of weeding out the poor performers and cancers.

There was also a continuing process of identifying the "stars" in the organization and those with potential beyond their current position. You need to take care of your stars – nurture them, make sure they're challenged and adequately compensated.

Getting the right reporting structure in place also was a challenge and required some fine tuning. The process of improving labor productivity continued. I placed a lot of emphasis on demand scheduling, which is simply the scheduling of employees to meet the demands of the business, with more front line employees working at peak times and fewer during the down times.

I trained the department managers to use internal reports that measure the business volumes for every hour of the day, as tools to determine how many employees they needed in each job classification for each hour of the day and day of the week. They then compared these "theoretical" staffing estimates to the actual number of employees they had scheduled, and we discovered that every department was overstaffed, some more than others of course.

Scheduling is a sensitive area, because of the way it affects people's lives, and also because it is so important to maximizing labor productivity. For those reasons, it always seems like that department, in any company, has an inordinate number of problems and issues to deal with.

The most opportunity for favoritism is in Scheduling. Trying to keep everybody happy is an impossible task. Trying to ensure that it is done fairly is an impossible task, but it is a goal that must be pursued.

Demand scheduling is Management 101 – pretty basic stuff. I discovered that a lot of the management team, at all levels, needed some basic training in many areas of the business. I spent a lot of time teaching not only demand scheduling, but also establishing goals and objectives, controlling overtime, evaluating performance, establishing accountability, etc.

Exhibits 36 – 41 give you a more in depth look at the issues, problems and challenges I dealt with, and how they were resolved. You will see the progress made in all areas of the business during this six week period. Probably the most gratifying improvement was in the morale. I know the front line employees liked what I was doing; management not so much, because they were being held accountable for performance. I've also included a report that quantifies the labor productivity improvement in the first three months.

In performing a turnaround, or any job for that matter, it's important to measure your results. Somebody famous once said, "You can't manage what you don't measure." You should find ways to measure everything you do – all areas of the business. Otherwise how do you know if you're improving?

By now I had a familiarization with, if not an intimate knowledge, of the entire management team (33 directors and managers). I had enough information to compile a short profile on each of them, and enough insight to classify them in one of four categories: 1) Seasoned veterans, 2) those who were recently promoted and already performing at a high level, 3) those who were recently promoted and have potential, but need development, and 4) those who are performing adequately, but could improve with better guidance and direction. This list is Exhibit 42.

It's important that you get to know everybody on the management team. A list like this can be useful, and it should be updated periodically. For each person reporting to you, you want to know who the potential replacements are. You want to know who the best candidates are for special projects. You want to know who to go to for information or assistance when their boss is not available.

The turnaround still didn't feel like it was completed. There was just too much work to do, so many opportunities for improvement. The results had become obvious to everybody, especially when the impact showed up on the bottom line. The improvement in morale was also obvious to everyone.

Apparently word of the turnaround had gotten out. I got a call from Rick Hilton. He had a buyer for the property.

Exhibit 36

Page 1 of 2

greg violette

From:	"greg violette" <gviovegas@lvcm.com>
To:	"Michael Paulson" <JMICHAELPA@aol.com>
Sent:	Sunday, April 06, 2003 9:42 PM
Subject:	Activity Report - Week of March 31

Mike,

I have launched a new initiative, a "second front" in the War on Wasteful Spending. This one involves all other operating expenses, besides labor. The Purchasing Manager tells me that we often pay more because of poor planning - last minute purchases. We also pay more because of people insisting on using a specific vendor, even though they may be more expensive. She has devised new forms to report these exceptions. The exceptions will be presented in the Executive Committee Meetings, and the Managers and Directors will be held accountable.

This is my approach to problem solving. I focus on the problem, by communicating the policies, expectations and rules to be followed to all management personnel involved. Then I get the key people who are involved to report exceptions. The exceptions are presented in the Executive Committee Meetings. The Managers and Directors get tired of being humiliated in front of their peers, and they take action to fix the problems. To solve the problem you have to hold people accountable, then confront each instance of abuse.

We have appointed Acting Managers in Surveillance and Security, after soliciting and interviewing interested people from within the departments. We are searching for a Director of Security and Surveillance. The two groups are meeting once or twice a week to evaluate policies and procedures and propose changes that will make the departments more efficient. The two groups are highly motivated, and I expect their proposals to include some positive changes.

There is some cancer in the Valet Department. We need to terminate a couple people, and perhaps change the reporting, so that Valet and Porters report to Security. They are in a better position to manage those people than the Hotel Director.

John Strickland, Director of Hotel Operations, was in the hospital for a week (again), and we are seeking a replacement for him.

John Maskovich, F&B Director, has completed his demand scheduling project in the Beverage Department. He is the only Director/Manager who really understands demand scheduling. His new schedules for Beverage Servers, Bartenders, Barbacks, and Bar Porters includes labor savings and provides for better customer service. He is initiating the process to solicit bids for the new schedules. It will take about a month to complete the process.

I have asked John to educate the rest of the management team, using his schedules, and the process he went through, as an example. I can talk 'til I'm blue in the face about the theory, but it will be more effective to use real examples. His presentation will be the focus of our meeting with all managers and supervisors on April 17.

We have some plans to increase gaming revenues:
1) We are introducing Keno in the Cafe.
2) We have a number of new promotions planned for Table Games.
3) I am working with the Poker Department to increase their revenues.

We have an opportunity to increase productivity in Housekeeping. The manager and supervisors have offered to increase the standard from 16 rooms to 18 rooms per employee, per shift. Their payroll and benefits are close to $2 million per year, and we have an opportunity to save more than $150,000 annually. I will be submitting a detailed proposal next week.

I am taking my message to the Hourly Employees. I am asking them to change. In order to understand the need to change, they need to know how bad it was. So I am telling them how dysfunctional the organization was (wasteful spending, favoritism, no accountablility, low standards, poor work ethic, etc). They deserve to know the truth. They need to know where we're heading and what our plans are. I am also telling them that our new focus is

4/6/2003

on them - increasing their job satisfaction. Most of them know how bad it was, and they appreciate that management is aware of the problems, and taking action to correct them. I am getting very positive feedback, after making the presentation to Housekeeping, Beverage Servers, Engineering and Pit employees. I have four meetings scheduled next week for all the rest of the hourly employees in groups of 200-250.

Hope to see you next week,
Greg

4/6/2003

Exhibit 37

Page 1 of 2

Greg Violette

From: "Greg Violette" <gviovegas@riverpalms.net>
To: <JMICHAELPA@aol.com>
Sent: Friday, April 18, 2003 2:08 PM
Subject: Activity Report - Week of April 14

Mike,

I completed an analysis of the first quarter income statement. I am thrilled that we were able to attain record revenues and profits during this difficult period of change and turmoil. I have some minor concerns that were addressed with individual department heads.

Demand scheduling is being implemented in all departments. Some departments are going through a bidding process to assign the new shifts to employees. It has been an eye-opening experience for most of them. After adjusting their schedules, they are finding that they have too many people to fit the new schedule, and the extra bodies can be eliminated through attrition. It is also giving us more staffing during peak periods, which will result in better customer service.

My focus on overtime is paying dividends also. The overtime hours for the first seven pay periods of the year averaged 1,723, with the highest being 2,584 and the most recent 2,142, until last pay period when it was only 846, less than half of what we have been averaging. If we can keep the overtime under 1,000 hours per pay period, the annual savings will be at least $250,000.

We had a meeting yesterday with all managers, supervisors and salaried personnel (over 100). I emphasized that the organization is now profitable and getting healthy - an amazing turnaround in ninety days. The layoffs are over, and we can now focus on getting stronger, by increasing productivity and reducing operating expenses.

I made it very clear that my expectations for the management team are:
1) Practice Common Sense Management techniques
2) Raise the performance standards
3) Practice demand scheduling
4) Implement accountability in their departments
5) Control overtime
6) Operate their departments with integrity, professionalism, honesty, fairness and consistency

I emphasized that we have brought nobody in from outside. A lot of people have been promoted, and are being given an opportunity to be successful. I am supporting them. Everybody who works hard and has a positive attitude has a chance to grow within the organization.

I have gotten a lot of positive feedback from that meeting and the ones last week with the hourly employees.

Wright and I had motivational meetings last week with the Hotel Director and Marketing Director, who were not meeting expectations. They now seem to be on track, and more in tune with what they should be doing.

The Surveillance Department has completed its reorganization plan. The Table Games Department has completed its Revenue Enhancement Plan.

Two engineers were laid off and won't be replaced. They were cancers. The Engineering Secretary position was eliminated. The employee will be transferred to another department, which has an opening. A Beverage Supervisor was terminated for performance issues. She will be replaced. An employee leaving the Uniforms Department will not be replaced. They were overstaffed.

The two Beverage Servers who have outstanding EEOC claims were terminated. They were cancers in the organization. They were warned a few weeks ago, with written disciplinary notices, to stop the intimidation and creating a hostile working environment for their co-workers. The practice continued. We worked very closely with our attorneys to ensure it was handled properly. It resulted in an immidiate morale boost to the entire Beverage

4/18/2003

89

Department and Pit employees.

The new standards in Housekeeping will be implemented in the next pay period.

We are geared up and well prepared for the River Run, our biggest week of the year.

Looking forward to your visit next week.

Greg

4/18/2003

**RIVER PALMS
CASINO*RESORT**

Memo

To: MIKE PAULSON

From: GREG VIOLETTE

Date: April 22, 2003

Re: LABOR PRODUCTIVITY

As you know we have eliminated approximately 5% of our labor force (about 60 jobs). However that does not tell the whole story about labor cost reduction. Our other efforts to reduce labor costs through demand scheduling, reducing overtime, etc. have paid dividends as well. The attached statistics point out the following facts:

1) Total labor hours were reduced (or productivity was increased) by 8% from the first pay period in January to the first pay period in April.

2) Overtime hours were reduced by 68% in the same time period.

3) Another way to measure productivity is a statistic called revenue per labor hour. It increased from $44.13 in January to $48.48 in March, a 10% increase in just two months.

The efforts continue, and the results speak for themselves.

1

Exhibit 39

Page 1 of 1

Greg Violette

From: "Greg Violette" <gviovegas@riverpalms.net>
To: <JMICHAELPA@aol.com>
Sent: Monday, April 28, 2003 12:28 PM
Subject: Activity Report

Mike,

As you know, the River Run was the primary focus of management last week. The Marketing Plan was in place long before my arrival, and I'm disappointed with the results. They keep making the same mistakes year after year. It will be done differently next year, if I'm still involved.

The Valet Department was very dysfunctional, and we now have a solution. There was a lot of favoritism, scheduling problems, etc., and it was all due to poor supervision. Ray Hernandez was a working bellman, and supervising both the Bell Desk and Valet. We demoted him to Lead Bellman (where he was before) and promoted Allyson Murray to Manager of Hotel Services.

Allyson was Manager of PBX, and has good supervisory skills. She is a disciplinarian, which is what the Valet Department needs. She now has responsibility for PBX, Valet and Bell Desk, and reports to the Hotel Director.

That was the last piece of the reorganization "puzzle". I'm confident now that we have the right people in the right places. The only remaining issue is the General Manager, and when that is resolved, defining Wright Wilson's responsibilities, and Dean Bridge's future.

The anxiety level has diminished substantially, and the morale is great. I'm getting a lot of positive feedback from the employees on the changes we've made and the direction we're headed. The only remaining anxiety has to do with the GM position, and my continuing role with the company.

We are finalizing the deal with Sun Country Airlines this week. We will buy fourteen seats a week on their flights originating in Dallas with intermediate stops. Our commitment is $3,000 per week for 16 weeks. They have committed to booking at least ten passengers a month into the River Palms from the Minneapolis-Denver route. Bob Daly, the Chairman of Sun Country, is a very good friend, and he has assured me that he will make sure this is a profitable venture for us. Our staff says it will be easy to fill the seats. This is not a big commitment, but I hope to build on it in the future.

The first few of a total of 24 foreign exchange students started working here last week. They are college students from Lithuania, who will be full time employees in Housekeeping and as Kitchen Workers. This is another Duff Taylor commitment, which makes no sense to me whatsoever. We just get done eliminating 60 jobs, and are going into the "slow" season, and we are forced to hire 24 new employees under a contract that he signed some time ago. Fortunately, they will all be working in high turnover positions.

I continue to address all the new hires each week in the Orientation classes. I'm continuing my focus on doing a better job of making the new employees feel welcome and comfortable. We are going to invite all new hires each month to the Employee of the Month Luncheon.

Wright and I met with a company from Vegas that is going to submit a proposal to use our Event Center as an arcade and entertainment center for teenagers for the summer months. The idea merits consideration.

Engineering has implemented a work order system, which will improve accountability and productivity.

Take care,
Greg

4/28/2003

Exhibit 40

Page 1 of 1

greg violette

From: "greg violette" <gviovegas@lvcm.com>
To: "Michael Paulson" <JMICHAELPA@aol.com>
Sent: Saturday, May 03, 2003 4:56 PM
Subject: Activity Report - Week Ending May 2, 2003

Mike,

Preliminary estimates indicate April revenues were about 1% lower than last year. One factor was a poor calendar, with only four Fridays, Saturdays and Sundays. I believe we did fairly well; and better than the competition, considering the war and high gas prices.

There was a lot of favoritism and unfairness in the scheduling of employees. We are in the process of revising the schedules to better reflect customer demand and improve productivity, and re-bidding them based on seniority to eliminate the prior inequities. This specifically applies to beverage servers, bartenders and pit employees. I am spending a lot of time reviewing and revising the schedules with the managers and having meetings with the employees to get their input. You get better employee satisfaction if you involve them in the process.

I have spent considerable time on the re-financing, but it appears that effort may have been wasted, considering the imminent sale of the property.

I am also reviewing all open requisitions for new emloyees (replacements), and many have been withdrawn by the department managers, after I review their schedules, and consider that business is now slowing down for the summer months. In other words I am making it difficult for managers to replace employees who leave. They must justify the need, and many of them have agreed that replacements are not needed at this time. And that is how we are futher reducing headcounts, and maintaining high levels of productivity through attrition.

I was able to cancel three of the foreign workers that were slated to be housekeepers. Two of them were transferred to the front desk, two are slated to be pool attendants, and one was assigned to be a houseman, to fill open positions. The disposition of the 12 kitchen workers, who haven't yet arrived, hasn't been determined. The F&B managers are evaluating the need. It is the highest turnover position that we have.

I now have the managers of Housekeeping, EVS (maintenance) and Kitchen employees working together to solve manpower requirements. It is part of my initiative to break down the walls between departments. All three of these departments employ workers specifically dedicated to cleaning, so it makes sense for them to cross-train and cross-utilize their employees. This has never been done in large casinos, but it makes sense, because small casinos do it all the time.

Next week I will start meeting with Directors and Department Managers to review and refine their goals and objectives, which were previously submitted. The meetings will also be used to give feedback on performance, agree on business strategies, and further communicate expectations. This will further solidify the accountability, which is now being implemented for the first time.

I am having difficulty scheduling meetings for next week, because of the Dragon Races. These are races between teams of employees from different casinos. The actual race will be held next weekend, but many of our employees are committed to several practice sessions that are being held throughout the week (they actually started last Thursday).
Our employees are manning two boats. I'm not sure we need to have two boats, or participate at all. This is another one of Wright Wilson's initiatives. He and Dean Bridge are leading the teams.

Looking forward to your visit next week,
Greg

5/3/2003

93

Exhibit 41

Greg Violette

From:	"Greg Violette" <gviovegas@riverpalms.net>
To:	<JMICHAELPA@aol.com>
Sent:	Friday, May 09, 2003 5:24 PM
Attach:	Headcount Trend Analysis.xls
Subject:	Weekly Activity Report - Week Ending 5/9/03

Mike,

I have been conducting departmental review meetings with all directors, department managers, and some supervisors. This week I met with Human Resources, Security, Surveillance, Slots, Pit, Poker, Bingo, Race/Keno, Environmental Services, Front Desk, Hotel Services (PBX, Valet & Bell Desk), Reservations, Housekeeping/Uniforms, Sales, Culinary, Restaurants, Beverage and Banquets. Next week I will complete the review process with Finance, Marketing and Engineering.

The purpose of the meetings is to ensure that the directives given to top level management have been implemented at the department level. I am reviewing and modifying schedules to ensure that demand scheduling has been implemented and staffing is being reduced for the summer season. I am reviewing labor cost management to ensure that overtime is being reduced and early outs are being managed properly. Goals and objectives are being reviewed and modified to ensure that accountability is being implemented and we have a basis for evaluating the performance of all management personnel. Organizational charts are being reviewed to determine that we have the most efficient use of personnel. Individual departments are documenting all the changes that have been implemented to improve efficiency, productivity, and reduce expenses. Dozens, if not hundreds, of procedures have been changed.

I am also using the meetings to seek justification for replacing employees who have recently quit. I was able to reduce the open requisitions for new employees from 57 to 22.

The process also allows me to evaluate the department managers, determine if they need further motivation, and identify those that have potential beyond their current level of responsibility.

It was brought to my attention that we have purchased 69 chef's white coats that are no longer of any use, because they had individual names (first and last) embroidered on them. That practice has been discontinued.

I have researched your inquiry about wage comparisons to last year. If you analyze the Headcount Trend Analysis that I have attached, it explains why there doesn't seem to be much improvement.

The fact is we have made significant reductions in labor costs since January, but the employee headcounts have only recently been reduced below the level of employees we had last year.

Headcounts were dramatically reduced in July of 2001, when revenues dropped significantly. The headcount levels stayed below 1,000 until January of 2002. Then they increased almost every month from 993 to 1,082 in December of last year. May is the first month this year that we have less people than the same month last year. However, you have to reduce the headcounts in 2003 by 27 - the number of employees in Pasta Cucina (or add 27 to last year's numbers) to be comparing apples to apples. So it actually was March when we first dropped below last year (right after the initial lay-offs). But it is not much below last year, with the extra people in Past Cucina. So if we maintain the current level of staffing for the rest of this year, the change compared to last year becomes more dramatic as the year progresses, especially in July, when headcounts really got out of hand last year.

The fact is that the big increase in EBITDA that we saw in the first quarter, compared to last year, was primarily due to higher revenues. The benefit of the lower labor costs will be more obvious as the year progresses.

Looking forward to your visit on Monday,
Greg

5/9/2003

94

Exhibit 42

RIVER PALMS RESORT * CASINO
Key Management Employees
Performance Assessment

SEASONED VETERANS

CFO & Acting Assistant General Manager – Wright Wilson, Age 43 – 3 years' service. Excellent Knowledge of property, market & competition. Enthusiastic, dedicated. Strong in Accounting, Marketing & IT.

Manager of Environmental Services (property maintenance) - Paul Williamson, age 61 - 3 years' service. Background in factory production management. Prior experience with Harrah's. Excellent all-around manager.

Manager of Housekeeping and Uniforms - Elizabeth Sealy, age 60 - 5 years' service. 20 years previous experience in housekeeping management with Sheraton, Red Lion and Beverly Manor. Excellent motivator.

Executive Chef - Boyzie Milner, age 49 - 9 months' service. Excellent technical skills. 8 years previous experience as Executive Chef in casinos.

Manager of Payroll – Julie Moody, age 49 - 19 years' service. 11 years in current position. High level of dedication. Has contributed greatly to labor cost savings initiative.

Manager of Purchasing – Roxanne Luna, age 41 – 14 years' service. High level of dedication. High level of integrity.

Manager of Bingo - Lillian Hatchett, age 52 – 19 years' service. Supervisor for 7 years, manager for last 8. Excellent results. Most profitable Bingo operation in the State of Nevada.

Operations Controller – Sharon Fortier, CPA, age 51 – 4 years' service. 2 years in current position. Potential to excel even more.

Financial Controller – Joe Wickam, age 59 – 4 years' service. 2 years in current position. Potential to excel even more.

Manager of Restaurants (Café & Pasta Cucina) – Deborah Bell, age 53 – 1 year service. 10 years experience as Restaurants Director at the Flamingo.

Manager of the Buffet – Maggie Sheppard, age 48 – 3 years service. High level of dedication. Good work ethic. Very good attention to detail.

MANAGERS/DIRECTORS WHO WERE RECENTLY PROMOTED, AND ARE ALREADY PERFORMING AT A HIGH LEVEL

Director of Gaming – Dean Bridge, Age 44 – 3 years' service. Excellent Slots knowledge & experience. Solid background.

Director of Food & Beverage – John Maskovich, Age 37 – 9 months' service. Extensive casino F&B experience. Good leader, well organized, follows directions well. Potential beyond current level of responsibility.

Manager of Human Resources – Jeanne Patskan, Age 43 – 7 years' service. 18 years in health care industry. High level of dedication. Good technical skills. Good leadership skills. Well respected. Well organized.

Manager of Slots – Ed Ailstock, age 42 - 2 years' service. Potential beyond current level of responsibility.

Manager of Surveillance – Jim Vollaire, age 60 – 6 years' service. Solid background in law enforcement and operations security in the aerospace industry. Potential beyond current level of responsibility.

Manager of Banquets – Jeannie Ferguson, age 56 – 1 year service. Extensive experience in local gaming market. High level of dedication. Good administrative and organizational skills.

MANAGERS/DIRECTORS WHO WERE RECENTLY PROMOTED AND HAVE POTENTIAL, BUT NEED DEVELOPMENT

Director of Marketing – Janette Hallmark, age 43 – 5 years' service in the number 2 spot. 15 years prior experience in advertising/marketing – five in a similar position with one of our competitors.

Manager of Engineering – Ron Valentine, age 51 – 15 year's service. High level of dedication. Good technical skills. Needs help with management skills.

Manager of Reservations & Front Desk – Barbara Harmon, age 52 – 10 years' service. High level of dedication. Needs guidance and direction.

Manager of Security – Bob Martin, age 45 – 3 years' service. Good background in private security. Highly motivated. Well respected. Needs guidance.

Manager of Hotel Services (Valet, Porters, PBX) – Allyson Murray, age 44 – 13 years' service. Highly motivated. Needs guidance and direction. Management skills are basically good, just needs refinement.

Manager of Table Games – Rob Pettit, age 34 – 7 years' service. Good technical skills. Needs direction, guidance and help with management skills.

Manager of Players' Club – Andre VanderVeldon, age 40 – 2 years' service. Potential beyond current level of responsibility. Needs guidance and direction.

Manager of The Lodge – Lynda Barela, age 53 – 5 months' service. Good background in food service. Needs guidance, direction and development of management skills.

Manager of Beverage Service – Mark Heaney, age 33 – 1 year service. Needs help with management skills.

Director of Hotel Operations – John Strickland, age 33 – 3 years' service. Previously served as Director of Marketing. Has potential, but needs to be replaced for health reasons.

EXISTING MANAGERS WHO ARE PERFORMING ADEQUATELY, BUT COULD IMPROVE WITH BETTER GUIDANCE & DIRECTION

Manager of Keno/Race Book – Renee Garland, age 52. 19 years service. Supervisor for 9 years, manager for last 3.

Manager of Information Technology – Steve Richards, age 36. 2 years's service.

Manager of Entertainment – Nancy Novak, age 34 – 4 years' service.

Manager of Advertising – Robert DelaRosa, age 26 – 1 year service.

Manager of Group Sales – Nicole Roselund, age 39 – 1 year service.

Manager of Poker – Ann Martin-Whitney, age 44 – 5 years' service.

KEY STATISTICS

AVERAGE AGE – 46

AVERAGE TENURE OF F&B MANAGEMENT (7) – 12 MONTHS

AVERAGE TENURE OF ALL OTHERS – 7.0 YEARS

HALF OF THE MANAGEMENT TEAM (16 OF 33) HAVE BEEN IN THEIR CURRENT POSITION LESS THAN THREE MONTHS

THE SALE

"My greatest satisfaction came from the troops."

Rick Hilton called in early May to tell me that Columbia-Sussex Corp. (CS) had made a full price, all cash offer, subject to due diligence. He asked me to "show" the property to the prospective owners, and provide them with all the information they need to make a final decision. I said I would be very cooperative, ensure that my staff is cooperative, provide them all the information they need, and put a positive spin on the operation.

CS is a privately owned Midwestern company that was successful over a long period of time in the hotel business. It was still owned by the same guy that started the company many years ago, and he had been very successful expanding the company internationally. His son was a partner now, and they made a strategic decision to become a player in the casino business (a good decision at that time). They also determined that buying the River Palms for $25 million was a bargain (a correct evaluation).

I met the father-son team at the first meeting in my office, and never saw them again. I got the impression that the son was kind of dragging his father reluctantly into this new business "arena." They dove into the gaming business head first. After buying the River Palms, they bought a smaller Las Vegas Off-Strip resort then they bought both Tropicana's – Las Vegas and Atlantic City. That was considered a "dive into the deep end" by many industry insiders, and nobody knew for sure if they could swim.

These guys did not seem to be interested in my opinions about the property or the market. They were very arrogant. They really didn't want any help or advice - "just give us the documents." I thought it was a strange attitude coming from guys who had never worked in or owned a casino.

Satisfying their due diligence requests was a big project – tax returns, financial statements, payroll records, etc. for several previous years. I made it a team project and split the tasks among my staff. CS sent their experts from every area of the business to meet with their counterparts at the River Palms, and learn how we did things in the casino business. It was time-consuming for many of us and a big distraction to the entire organization. However, I took responsibility for keeping the buyer happy and ensuring a smooth transition.

The hardest thing to get used to, and the biggest impediment for newcomers (owners) to the business, is the high level of regulation. The licensing process is lengthy, expensive and intrusive. The State Gaming Commission, in every jurisdiction, keeps a close eye on the casinos. Their agents roam around the state. In some states they carry weapons. In a way, the casinos are like banks, with strict controls on cash handling and access, and reporting large and suspicious transactions to the IRS. It is a big adjustment for many, especially the entrepreneurial types.

The news of the sale was a shock to all of us. There were never any rumors that someone had an interest, and all of sudden there was a buyer! Rick Hilton told me about a month later that he subsequently received four backup offers... WOW!

I knew within thirty minutes of meeting the buyers that there was no chance of either Wright Wilson or me staying on as the General Manager. That was disappointing to me. I really would have enjoyed that. It was the best job I ever had. I had already proven myself and gained the respect of the troops. But of course, I never revealed to anyone my true feelings about that.

There were some nice perks to go along with my position there. The downside is that it was like living in a fish bowl. Of course, the employees watched my every move. I was somewhat used to that, but it is magnified when you live on the property. I've never complained about that. I enjoyed mingling with the employees and customers. I tried to make that a high priority. It's easy to get stuck in your office for days at a time, if you allow that to happen.

My greatest satisfaction came from the troops. They expressed their respect and admiration for me with their words, and I could see it in their eyes. That is what I missed the most, along with helping people develop and watching them grow.

Wright Wilson's hopes of becoming the General Manager faded with time. He, along with everyone else, focused his efforts on keeping his job – any job. Wright was going to lose his job no matter what happened because if the place hadn't sold, I would have terminated him eventually. He just had too much baggage. He never gained the respect of the troops.

Exhibit 43 is a summary of a departmental reorganization, which will give you some insight into my approach.

Exhibits 44 – 47 are my Activity Reports for the previous thirty days. You can see that most of my efforts are geared toward the transfer of ownership.

Exhibit 48 is a complimentary letter from an employee.

Exhibit43

**RIVER PALMS
RESORT * CASINO**

Memo

To: MIKE PAULSON

From: GREG VIOLETTE

CC: JOE YUNG, HOWARD REINHARDT

Date: June 6, 2003

Re: GROUP SALES REORGANIZATION

I recognized early in my operational review an opportunity to improve Group Sales. Last year they did approximately $850,000 in sales with a fairly high profit margin. The facilities for meetings, banquets, trade shows, etc. are significantly under-utilized. We have a great venue for weddings, but we have never made a serious attempt to go after that business. I believe we could increase sales 50% quite easily, with the potential to at least double it.

I also learned during my review that the operational part of Group Sales - actually delivering the product, coordination, service, etc. - was very dysfunctional. The responsibility for banquets had bounced around from Hotel to Marketing to Food & Beverage. In January, Paul Williamson was the Banquets Manager. He was also the Manager of Environmental Services (janitorial services). Paul is one of the best managers we have, and that is why he was given responsibility for banquets (because it was dysfunctional), but he was admittedly out of his league in that area.

In late February we relieved Paul of his responsibilities as Banquets Manager and promoted Jeannie Ferguson, who had been the Marketing Promotions Coordinator, a position that was eliminated. She had some prior experience in Banquets at another local casino, and is one of our star performers. She reports directly to the F & B Director, where that responsibility belongs. Those organizational changes have resulted in a significant improvement in Banquet operations.

However, other operational problems have come to light recently that involve contractual, coordination and service issues. My analysis of the problems revealed that these issues are resulting from the fact that the booking and coordination of the banquets is done by Group Sales, which reports to the

1

Hotel Director. To correct these operational problems, and to accomplish my other goal of increasing sales, I made the following changes this week:

1) Created a position called Banquets Sales Coordinator, which reports directly to the F&B Director, but acts as liaison between Group Sales and the Banquets Manager. This is an administrative and coordination position, but also includes insides sales. Taking this responsibility away from the Group Sales Manager will ensure better coordination and service, allow the Group Sales Manager to focus more on sales, and create an inside sales function.

2) Dixie Oropeza was appointed to the position of Banquets Sales Coordinator. She has prior experience in that area with other local casinos. Her current position as Sales Coordinator in the Tour & Travel Department (busing) has been eliminated, because of a reduction in business volume.

3) Debbie Bolton, Manager of the Tour & Travel Department, has been authorized to spend more time traveling (trade shows) to promote the River Palms and increase sales.

4) To improve coordination and service, Dixie will be physically located in the Group Sales office, Jeannie Ferguson will move into the F&B office, and Jeannie's old office in Marketing will be turned into a "showroom" to entertain prospective clients/customers and make sales pitches.

With these changes I'm confident that we will achieve our goals of increasing sales and improving efficiency and service. All people involved are happy with the changes, and are highly motivated to help us reach our true potential in the area of Group Sales.

Exhibit 44

Page 1 of 1

Greg Violette

From: "Greg Violette" <gviovegas@riverpalms.net>
To: <JMICHAELPA@aol.com>
Sent: Friday, May 16, 2003 2:03 PM
Subject: Activity Report - Week Ending 5/16

Mike,

My primary focus this week was preparing the Due Diligence book (Disclosure Schedule) for Columbia-Sussex, and reviewing the Purchase Agreement. Spent considerable time on the phone with Dave Whittemore and his associates.

I had Departmental Review meetings with all the Marketing Departments - Player's Club, Entertainment, Direct Mail, Advertising, and Player Development, as well as Engineering. I am establishing goals and objectives at the department level, defining expectations, doing some strategic planning and providing feedback on performance.

I also had meetings with Group Sales, Banquets and the Tour & Travel Departments. We are making some organizational changes to place more emphasis on Sales and improve our operational performance in the Banquets Department.

The Reservations Manager was given responsibility for the Front Desk as well, to plug a hole that we have had for a few weeks.

We got the April Financial Statements this week. Gaming revenue was flat with last year. Total revenue was off 2% from last April. I believe that is mostly due to a poor calendar, and I believe we are still out-performing the market on revenues. EBITDAR was down $180,000 from last year, but we are still $829,000 ahead of last year for the YTD period. For the first 14 days of May, our total revenues are 6% ahead of last year.

Columbia-Sussex will have two guys on site next week to look at F& B. I will ensure that they are treated well, and get all the information they need.

Take care,
Greg

Exhibit 45   Page 1 of 1

Greg Violette

From:	"Greg Violette" <gviovegas@riverpalms.net>
To:	<JMICHAELPA@aol.com>
Sent:	Friday, May 23, 2003 4:35 PM
Subject:	Activity Report - Week Ending 5/23

Mike,

Spent the majority of the week entertaining/educating two representatives of Columbia-Sussex (CS), who specialize in F&B and Hotel Operations, and preparing for the visit of nine more representatives of CS next week.

Also:
1) Had a meeting with a company proposing a barter program.
2) Met with F&B and Purchasing management to help resolve differences. Concluded that the problem is mainly lack of communication. Solution was to establish a meeting schedule (twice a week).
3) Met with the Surveillance Team to review progress, establish guidelines, and reinforce the Manager's authority and my support for him.
4) Met with Beverage Department to make decisions on questions of seniority before the bidding process on the new schedules commences.
5) Entertained the consultant hired by CS to perform an Environmental Assessment.

Other concerns, issues and notable items were discussed in our phone conversations.

Greg

5/23/2003

Exhibit 46

Page 1 of 1

Greg Violette

From:	"Greg Violette" <gviovegas@riverpalms.net>
To:	<JMICHAELPA@aol.com>
Sent:	Friday, May 30, 2003 3:09 PM
Subject:	Activity Report - Week Ending 5/30

Mike,

Most of my time this week was devoted to the due diligence by Columbia-Sussex - educating the nine people who were on property this week, as well as follow up questions after they left. Most of the feedback I have gotten from our people that spent time with them was that "it's a done deal".

I have faxed the Dave Coffey contracts - Gift Shop and Arcade to Dave Whittemore. Should have a Notice of Default by Tuesday.

Spent some time on restructuring personnel and responsibilities within the Tour & Travel, Group Sales, and Banquets Departments.

Will have preliminary revenue numbers for May early next week. I remain optimistic about the May results.

Hope to see you next week,
Greg

Exhibit 47

Page 1 of 1

Greg Violette

From:	"Greg Violette" <gviovegas@riverpalms.net>
To:	<JMICHAELPA@aol.com>
Cc:	"Howard Reinhardt" <hreinhardt@horizoncasino.com>; "Joe Yung" <joeyung@ix.netcom.com>
Sent:	Monday, June 09, 2003 3:02 PM
Subject:	Activity Report - Week Ending 6/8

Mike,

Spent most of my time last week reorganizing Group Sales and Front Services. Have sent you the details on those changes.

Performed an inventory of Allen Paulson's sports memorabilia, which will be excluded from the sale.

Reviewed F&B staffing with F&B Director, HR Manager and CFO.

Worked with attorney to prepare Notice of Default on Gift Shop and Arcade. Letter was sent to Dave Coffey late last week.

Two barbacks and two banquet porters were terminated for disciplinary reasons.

Changed method of selecting Employee of the Month, and also changed awards for all twelve nominees (no additional expense). Starting in June it will be a dinner, rather than luncheon, and will be followed by a sunset cruise on the Del Rio (no cost).

Continued providing documentation to Columbia-Sussex.

John Strickland (Hotel Director) has missed three weeks in a row now since his hospitalization, not counting one week he missed in April. Will consult with new owners before replacing him.

June revenue is soft for the first week, compared to last year. We are doing everything possible to fill the rooms, but I expect revenue in June to be weak, because of a poor calendar.

Take care,
Greg

6/9/2003

106

Exhibit 48

Greg Violette

From:	Casino Operations
Sent:	Thursday, June 05, 2003 5:08 PM
To:	Greg Violette
Subject:	Comment

Hi Greg -

When you announed in the last Managers meeting that you would be staying at River Palms, I personally was very pleased. I feel that you are a very focused person whose main concern is the operations of this casino and the treatment of employees. You have no idea how refreshing that is. You earned respect in every department in a very short period of time - a very difficult feat at this casino. And now I am concerned that you will be leaving when (and if) the new owners take over. I would hope you don't, as everything you have acommplished has turned out for the best. Morale is so much better!

But, if it turns out that you must leave, I want you to know that I have a great deal of respect for your abilities and consider it a privilige to work with you. Thanks for being here at such a critical time.

Kay Meggison

6/5/2003

THE CLOSING

I was told that the buyer wanted me to refrain from making any more operational, structural or organizational changes - understandable I guess. I continued my coaching, teaching, and fine tuning. But I definitely took my foot off the gas. I felt like I had my hands tied. It was then that I realized I had "worked myself out of a job."

I knew the deal was going to close when CS started spending money on the facility. They started working first on the things they know best, like Housekeeping. They converted an area in the basement, previously used by the Facilities Department, into a Laundry. Hotel people know laundry!

They had jackhammers going all day long. It was noisy, dirty and disruptive. Morale plummeted, and people were in fear of losing their job. It was not a fun place to work anymore. The closing was scheduled for September 8. Business dropped. It was a long summer.

Transferring ownership of a casino is tricky. It takes a lot of planning. At midnight we had to take inventory of everything, from cash and chips to food and beverage – without closing the casino.

One thing that was excluded from the sale was Allen Paulson's collection of sports memorabilia, which was on display behind locked cases in the Sports Book. There were baseballs, footballs, basketballs, hockey sticks, soccer balls, jockeys' caps, and much more. All of them signed by somebody famous. Michael asked me to take possession of those items until he could find a place to store them. I had a couple of employees use a company van to transport it to my home in Henderson.

All that stuff, along with the 15' by 30' tapestry portrait of Cigar, rolled up like a carpet, sat in my garage for three or four months, until Michael sent somebody to pick it up. I was hoping he would forget about it, but he said something about "giving it to the grandkids" (his children, nieces and nephews).

The closing went smoothly, but there was one thing that really upset Michael in the final days. Before my arrival, Wright had signed a five-year contract with a commercial laundry company. He did that knowing the property was for sale! CS built a laundry facility, and wouldn't accept that contract obligation. Michael had to eat about $500,000. He had good reason to be upset.

The last time I saw Wright Wilson was the day of the Closing. In a meeting with Michael, Wright asked him for a bonus – "Do you think Greg and I can get a little something for helping you close this deal?" I was very surprised to hear that. He had never mentioned anything to me about a bonus.

After taking advantage of the Company for so long, I thought it took a lot of nerve for him even to ask. His timing was also terrible. As Michael kind of turned his back on Wright, shaking his head, I heard him mumble something about "$500,000" and a "laundry contract."

I learned a long time ago that if you don't have leverage; it's not negotiating, it's begging. After the turnaround is complete is not the time to ask for a bonus. It was a mistake, though, not to include a Success Fee in my contract proposal. It is pretty standard - a turnaround incentive to get the place sold. Michael probably wouldn't have blinked if I asked for 1% of the sale price if the property is sold within one year - stupid me!

I didn't even think about the Success Fee because I was thrilled to get my dream job with a big salary and perks. I also felt a little guilty, because I didn't have to work very hard the last three months. It was still a mistake – I should have asked for the bonus up front.

For the next few weeks, I did a little part time work for Michael, cleaning up loose ends, primarily trying to collect his debts. It gave me something to do while I was searching for the next gig. This last one didn't last very long, but I really enjoyed the ride!

POSTSCRIPT

"I wasn't sure if he just called me a liar or said that I accomplished the impossible."

Most of the Directors were terminated or left within the first year under the new owners. I had cut the fat out of the organization, but CS went even deeper - right to the bone, and it impacted customer service and satisfaction. Revenues dropped dramatically. Their casinos in Las Vegas and Atlantic City were also failures. They just never figured out that you can't run a casino like a hotel.

I knew they were doomed when the first General Manager they appointed for the River Palms was our HR Manager. I was shocked that it wasn't somebody from the outside, and shocked that it was her. She was a nice lady, but had little knowledge of how a casino is operated.

I think they just wanted someone who would follow orders – a good soldier that wouldn't question anything they were doing. They eventually either sold or lost all four casinos, when they went into bankruptcy. What a shame to take all those employees down that path!

At a casual lunch with one of the CS executives, I explained the challenges I faced with the turnaround. He said, "You can't make all those changes at once – it's too disruptive to the organization. You have to change one thing at a time, and give the employees a chance to assimilate." I didn't respond, because I wasn't sure if he just called me a liar or said that I accomplished the impossible.

About four months after the September 8 Closing, I got a call from Michael Paulson, "Greg, you ready to tackle Full House Resorts?" I answered, "You bet, let's do it!"

That would be the last project of my career – allowed me to retire early. It's an interesting story too… for another time.

ABOUT THE AUTHOR

Greg's journey started in the tiny town of Buhl, Minnesota, where he grew up in the north woods with miners and lumberjacks. He experienced a drastic change of culture in 1973, after graduating from the University of Minnesota, Duluth, when he moved from Buhl to Los Angeles to pursue his dream, since age 16, of becoming a corporate executive.

He spent the first half of his career working for big companies - GTE, Hertz and Northwest Airlines. At age 35 he was the CFO for the Western Region of Hertz Rent a Car, where he was second in command over 2,000 employees at 25 locations in the western states. At NWA he spearheaded a cost reduction initiative, while employed at their corporate headquarters.

Greg then got into the casino business, and worked as the CFO for four casinos in the Midwest and Colorado – two Indian casinos, one riverboat casino and one commercial casino. The last seven years of his career, he worked in Las Vegas as the CFO for Pacific Coast Gaming and Full House Resorts – casino management/ development companies.

In those seven years, he was involved in opening seven casinos in Washington and one in southern California, in addition to overseeing the management of five others. He hired and trained all the controllers for those properties. In total he was involved in nine startups and five turnarounds during his career.

In 2003 Greg directed a turnaround at the River Palms in Laughlin, Nevada - the subject of this book. That was his most challenging and his most rewarding job – the highlight of his career. He quit working three years later, after one more turnaround project, at the age of 56. Ten years later he decided to finish this book. He has now moved back to northern Minnesota, so it seems the circle is complete.

www.ingramcontent.com/pod-product-compliance
Lightning Source LLC
Chambersburg PA
CBHW060445240326
41598CB00087B/3483